MR. BROWN COMES DOWN THE HILL

Plays by Peter Howard

THE REAL NEWS
THE BOSS
THE DICTATOR'S SLIPPERS
WE ARE TOMORROW
PICKLE HILL
THE LADDER
THROUGH THE GARDEN WALL
THE DIPLOMATS

With Cecil Broadhurst

THE VANISHING ISLAND

With Anthony Howard

SPACE IS SO STARTLING

With Alan Thornhill

THE HURRICANE
MUSIC AT MIDNIGHT

MR. BROWN
COMES DOWN
THE HILL

By

PETER HOWARD

LONDON

BLANDFORD PRESS

FIRST PUBLISHED MAY 1964
BY BLANDFORD PRESS, LTD
167 HIGH HOLBORN, LONDON, W.C.1

PRINTED IN GREAT BRITAIN BY
W. & J. MACKAY & CO. LTD., CHATHAM

PREFACE

WHEN FIRST I SPOKE of this play to a friend, he said, "You will have trouble with censor and critics." As he, being famous, bears scar tissue on every part of his body from critics' tooth and claw, I heeded what he said. But I finished the play.

Now I want to say something about critics before they get their say at me. Many of them are honest. Some are not. In modern society, most young people are joy and glory. A minority, who smash windows, lecher and blaspheme, masquerade as members of the opposite sex, slash with knife, lash with chain, bully, brag and punch up the neighbourhood, make news and influence nations. So it is with critics.

Critics think themselves more formidable than any censor. In this they are right. Their weapon is a bomb. The censor only wields scissors. The censor can slash. Critics can destroy.

Yet I feel more kind to critics than to censor. I would use, if I could, the critics' bomb on the censor—and the censor's scissors on some of the critics. Perhaps it is because for many years I was a critic myself. I earned a living by dipping my pen in acid and sharpening my sword by plunging it into the leathery flanks and sandy entrails of public men.

Of course, fair critics are essential and valuable servants of art. But some critics are biased.

Criticism with bias is a deadly ailment. You may blast

other men's work and art with your bomb. But you destroy your soul as you do it.

Not that there is lack of honour in critics' work. If you fail, as many successful critics have failed, to earn a living painting pictures, playing music or writing books and plays yourself, there is no reason why you should not take money from those sanguine enough to pay it, for telling artists, writers and musicians how better to do the job that has beaten you.

But power corrupts. Critics have power. And some think their power greater than it is. Folk flatter them. Playwrights, eager for applause, praise them. Pride robs them of objectivity. It is easier to pull down than to build up, to destroy than to direct. Their names become better known to TV viewers or newspaper readers than those of artists whose work they bombard. They enjoy the wild glory of trampling on creations of their fellow men.

Criticism is strong drink. Few critics have stomach to swallow and stay sober. Many become drunken with power of destructiveness and, instead of remaining just, become creatures of prejudice.

They create a world of their own, live inside it and lose touch with humanity. It is a small world with a big voice. But the world of such critics could collapse quickly if their bluff were called and their false values challenged that they force upon the public. This sort of critic would resist the destruction of his tiny world. For power has glamour. Men fall in love with it. They come to think they are the cultural and artistic Hitlers of the land. As Hitler crammed Wagner into the jowls of the Germans while he munched cream buns, so some modern critics thrust Lenny Bruce and Tennessee Williams at us while teenagers in the audience nibble Purple Hearts, and elderly people suck tranquillisers.

With certain brave and noble exceptions, critics are prone to dictatorship. Hitler was a critic of the Jews. He demanded that all agree with him. The Austrian house-painter used all the filthy paraphernalia of Goebbels, Gestapo and gas chambers to force his views down the gullet of Germany. Germans began to gulp cruelty and hate.

In the same way, many modern British critics are dictators. If you do not drink, think, wanton and sneer at virtue as they do, they use gas on the air, lies on the public platform, ink on paper to bully Britain in their direction. Britain, to her shame, has allowed herself to be bullied a long way the wrong way. We are a nation of moral funks. We would rather keep good men silent or out than risk siding with them. We rightly blame the Germans for not defying Hitler's threats of physical violence and assassination. But we bow to the threats of character assassination and smear used by the pocket Hitlers and modern McCarthys of television, press and radio. We capitulate when told we will not get publicity, or that plays will not be produced unless we praise perversion and deify dirt.

In old days it was said, "Give a dog a bad name and hang him". Nowadays, it could be said, "Give a dog a good name—and persecute him, annihilate him, destroy him".

Some British critics not only become dictators. They

also become censors. The censorship they exercise in Britain today is subtle, sophisticated, far more perilous than that of the Lord Chamberlain. Shaw once said, "All censorships exist to prevent anyone from challenging current conceptions and existing institutions. All progress is initiated by challenging current conceptions and executed by supplanting existing institutions."

The current conception is that dirt on the stage is pay dirt and that violence, cynicism, and the twistier sides of the human heart are themes of best drama.

Sex is a part of life. It, therefore, has a part on the stage. But its part should be as a problem for thoughts and answers, not as a glamourised aphrodisiac with every oddity and quirk enlarged to rob the subject of proper shape and size.

The existing institution in British theatre, sustained by some critics, decrees that satirists, sexists and sadists with a few drunkards thrown in are often more certain of welcome as artists, actors, producers or writers than those who lead less exotic lives.

If this institution or conception is challenged, some critics first try to slay with silence. When that fails, they march to slaughter with smear. The censorship of these critics (as well as some producers in the BBC, ITV, stage and film studios) against faith and decency, and for cynicism, cruelty, class-war, nihilism, violence, filth and anti-Christ, is a most powerful censorship today. But it is the censorship of a minority. It is dictatorship. It can and must be ended.

For many reasons I am against censorship of all kinds, especially the kind created by this minority of modern critics. They, by the way, join in a chorus of loud shouts against the comparatively harmless slashes and jabs of the Lord Chamberlain who sometimes cuts this or that to prove he can earn the guineas he charges the unhappy author for mutilating his product. I am all for shouting at the Lord Chamberlain and taking away his scissors. But these critics who censor us all with their prejudices and perversions provide argument for the preservation of the Lord Chamberlain, scissors and all.

These minority critics are often so eager to censor and smash any play challenging their conceptions and institutions that they pretend to miss the point of the play itself. So for the benefit of any men of bias who may see or read *Mr. Brown Comes Down the Hill*, I would like to make one point of it plain.

It is in fact an attempt to show who are the Christ-killers of all times.

For centuries Christians have traded on the view that the Jews killed Christ. From time to time they have used blood and terror. Counting up all the massacres, all the miseries, all the degradations of the human spirit and heart in the last two thousand years, it is probable that Christians have persecuted Jews as brutally as did Hitler. The reason is a guilty conscience. For it is the Christians who continue to kill Christ.

The Roman soldiers did the actual killing. They were men under orders. No doubt, like Hitler's generals, though with truth, their defence would have been, "We knew nothing about it. We only did what we were told."

The Jews accused Christ of setting Himself up as King.

It was, in one sense, a true charge. Christ never offered any reasoned defence against it. He was Himself a Jew. And His challenge to current conceptions and existing institutions was not only inconvenient but dangerous to a race living under Roman military rule, and where the emergence of any King would have been put down with the ruthless might and brutality of Roman legions. Censorship of the Cross seemed to the Establishment of that time a reasonable answer to the challenge.

The Roman authorities did not take much trouble to understand the causes of disturbance. They wanted tranquillity in a small province where, if people kept quiet and there was no trouble, they might soon get home to the comforts, honours, promotions awaiting civil servants and soldiers who had served the Empire well. The crucifixion of Christ meant less to them than the hanging, on golf-courses in Kenya, of Mau Mau murderers meant to British authorities during the Emergency.

The real Christ-killers were supporters of Christ—snobs who came by night but turned aside in the daylight, a mob which cheered when things were going well and jeered when they went badly, close friends and supporters who ratted when enemies came to arrest Christ and take Him away.

It is true they had an excuse then which today is lacking. The crowds who surrounded Christ and acquiesced in his execution did not fully understand what he stood for or required of them. Peter had the guts to draw his sword and Christ told him to put it away again. He did not want men militant for the wrong thing.

Today Churchmen, most men, know in their hearts what Christ stands for and requires of them. But we prefer coronets to Calvary, public acclaim to the Cross. We choose soft respectability and funk hard fighting.

Yet even two thousand years ago, some knew the truth. If at that time the Nicodemuses and Gamaliels who knew the truth about Jesus had risked their necks and their repute to assert it, the tide of opinion would have turned against the men who were out to destroy Him. Patting on the back after nightfall does not prevent the crucifixion of good men on a hill in daylight. If the crowd had cheered Jesus, and kept on cheering, the Romans might never have sent Him to the Cross. If the few had stayed faithful and militant, the masses might have stuck to the man they admired. The Roman authorities only wanted to fulfil the will of the majority. Which they did.

Christians would say that without the betrayal and killing of Christ, there would have been no Calvary, no Redemption, no Resurrection. But it is hard to see why Christians all down the ages persist in the attitude that condemned Jesus to death. Some seem to think that if Christ had had a good public relations officer, He would not have been killed. It is a misreading of history. Christ was killed for what He was, not for what He was not. Christ, with His desire for perfection, His challenge, "Be ye perfect, even as your Father in Heaven is perfect", is an everlasting barb in the conscience of humanity. That is why today so many try to popularise Christ by attempting to diminish Him, to emasculate His absolute moral claims.

If Christ in the flesh came walking down Piccadilly, He would find friends among the people, rich men as well as poor, harlot and pervert as well as puritan and house-wife, teenage ton-uppers as well as elderly squares. But the Establishment, Left and Right, would find ways of killing Him and, with modern progress, killing Him fast. For Christ was and is and ever will be outside the control of any Establishment. This is something that Establish-ments, including established churches, cannot bear.

So for two thousand years, and in more than two thou-sand ways, millions of Christians have been crucifying Christ again. They have cut Him down from the Cross, cut Him up into manageable man-size packages, insisted on His conforming to their ways and shapes and sizes, put scores of different labels on Him and shocked humanity by anger, bitterness and violence if others do not recognise their part of the package as the only genuine article. If Christ had been like the Christians, nobody would have heard of Him. He would not have been worth the cost of trial and execution.

And those who, from the pulpit, pretend that Christ is *not* the same yesterday, today and for ever, and that His challenge must be cut to the comfort of modern man, with their determination to reject the moral absolutism of Jesus, crucify Him again, more dishonestly, more viciously than any Jew.

Now, there are four Protestant bishops in this play. The only passage cut from the text sent to the Lord Chamberlain was a speech made to me by one of the most prominent Anglican bishops of today.

My four bishops are not real bishops. If anyone thinks they are, he will judge the Church of England and also judge me. That is something the New Testament tells Christian men and women not to do. Real bishops are, for the most part, sincere and splendid men. Some, it is true, wear glory with an apologetic air that is the mark of one kind of humility. But it seems shameful to blame bishops if a negative minority among them grab headlines and make news, while a devout majority protest in muted tones and without much impact on modern society.

Protestant bishops should, of course, protest. They should protest more vehemently against the few among them who seem eager with doubtful disputations on theology to dispossess men of faith, and confuse a nation with justifications of infidelity and deviance. Today churchmen should find themselves persecuted for faithfulness to the Cross instead of praised and made popular for desertion of it.

But the bishops in this play are an image, an unjust image, a false image, a sort of comic cartoon created in the minds of millions of ordinary men by noisy attitudes and unhappy silences of some leaders of the Church of England. Many people have come to believe that Churches are determined to control the Holy Spirit instead of being controlled by Him. They sense a critical spirit about any work of God that happens outside the organisational walls. They suspect a narrowness of heart which believes that God is only respectable if He is safely imprisoned inside the Establishment. They think they detect in Christians great cowardice when faced with the right controversy but also much courage when it comes to accepting the wrong compromises. They have the idea that they are expected to live for the Churches instead of the Churches learning to live again for all the people.

It is this image, false if the desires and longings of most churchmen's hearts were fulfilled, which must be faced and altered. People are cool about the Church of England because they feel many of its members have become cool towards the absolute claims of Christ on the Cross, Who loves and challenges everybody on earth to carry it with Him.

Just as in this play the bishops are not real bishops, so the pressmen are not real pressmen. Pressmen in Britain are more honest than most of those they write about. They have a capacity for hard work, without regular hours or overtime pay, that would make Britain lick the earth in production if it were applied in industry. They give the public what they think the public want. Some of them secretly despise the public for wanting it. Be this said to the everlasting credit of the Press. Some newspapers of Britain, in an age of slipping standards, have refused to yield to dirt as enthusiastically as television, radio and theatre.

The pressmen in the play are one part, one image of the Street of Ink. It is not a full picture of the Press. But it is as true a picture as that painted about events in some newspapers everyday.

The doctor, the black man, the harlot are not real in themselves. They are parts of every human heart. They are bits of you and me walking and talking before us. Like or dislike them, it is ourselves we survey.

Somebody asked the other day, "Why write plays?" Some write for money. Some for fame. Some, though very few, for art. They feel beauty in their guts which they have to display to others with paint, and the performance of skilled professionals on stage and screen. Some just write for fun.

These reasons are not mine. My ink is sweat. I do not find dipping in that pot funny. Fame is not for me and I do not take royalties from my plays. All winnings are given to charity.

I write to preach. I write for the sake of propaganda. I write with a message and for no other reason. Do not believe those who say the theatre is no place for a man with a message of some kind. Some writers give their message without knowing they do it. A man who writes as if life had no meaning is the man with a strong message.

Plays nowadays propagate sex, violence, cynicism and the debunking of patriotism. Love of country is distorted and made to seem folly. In other days the theatre preached ancient virtues, including patriotism of an unselfish sort, because it would have gone bankrupt had it not done so. The public expected morality on the stage. Shaw, Galsworthy, Ibsen, even Wilde and Lonsdale, were great moralisers of their times.

My plays are propaganda plays. I write them to give people a purpose. The purpose is clear. The aim is simple. It is to encourage men to accept the growth in character that is essential if civilisation is to survive. It is to help all who want peace in the world to be ready to pay the price of peace in their own personalities. It is to end the censorship of virtue which creates vicious society. It is to enlist everybody everywhere in a revolution to remake the world. It is, for Christians, the use of the stage to uplift the Cross and make its challenge and hope real to a perverse but fascinating generation.

Characters

BLACK MAN

HARLOT

BISHOP

MR. BROWN

ANDY

DOCTOR

FIRST PRESSMAN

SECOND PRESSMAN

SECOND BISHOP

THIRD BISHOP

FOURTH BISHOP

PRESSWOMAN

POLICEMAN

NEWSMAN

ACT ONE

ACT TWO

MR. BROWN COMES DOWN THE HILL was first produced in London at the Westminster Theatre, opening on 28 May 1964 with the following cast:

BLACK MAN	Mark Heath
HARLOT	Lillias Walker
BISHOP	John Richmond
MR. BROWN	Eric Flynn
ANDY	Alan White
DOCTOR	Richard Warner
FIRST PRESSMAN	Robert Hartley
SECOND PRESSMAN	Kenneth Waller
SECOND BISHOP	Bryan Coleman
THIRD BISHOP	Donald Simpson
FOURTH BISHOP	Noel Carey
PRESSWOMAN	Pauline Loring
FIRST POLICEMAN	Guy Standeven
SECOND POLICEMAN	Mike Lewin
PATRONS IN THE BAR	Gina Curtis
	Astley Harvey

Directed by Henry Cass
Settings by Hutchinson Scott
Lighting by Louis Fleming

ACT ONE

SCENE ONE

As the curtain rises, a steep hill can be seen. It leaps jaggedly in three tiers from the left until it disappears towards the sky on the right. The lower tier is largest and covers more than half of the stage. A black man is on the middle tier. He is stripped to the waist and sweating. He is shouting to some companion struggling up the hill who cannot at first be seen.

BLACK MAN Come on! (*To himself*) You lazy bitch. (*Shouts again*) Hurry!

VOICE OF A WOMAN (*From below*) What's the hurry? I don't think I'm going much farther. I'm tired.

BLACK MAN This is no time to be tired. I was a fool to bring you. Put your left foot on that rock. No. *Left* foot, idiot. There.

(As he calls to her, the Harlot comes into sight, scrambling on to the lower tier of the hill. She is climbing, but not dressed for it. Indeed, one reason for her slowness is that she seems unwilling to do anything that may disturb her clothes or her appearance)

HARLOT Just a minute. (*She pulls out a box of make-up and begins to use it*)

BLACK MAN Stop that. Stop it, I tell you.

HARLOT Bless your little black heart and bright brown eyes. We *are* in a state, aren't we? If you think you're going to get me further or faster by bullying me and turning as red in the face as a man like you can turn, you're crazy. Anyway, if I'm going to meet my Maker, or whatever it is you say we are going to do up there, I mean to meet Him looking my best. Manners don't cost much—even on mountains. And if I know anything about God, which I don't, He'll notice what I look like, which is more than can be said for you. (*She goes on making up*)

BLACK MAN I'm coming down. I'm going to give you something that'll make you jump and climb, my girl. Something that you'll not forget in a hurry. You'll need to make up something besides your face by the time I've finished with you.

(*The Black Man gestures as if to hit her and prepares to come down to her. She looks at him without concern. Then continues to make up her face*)

HARLOT Come down, by all means. It's time we all came down and went home, if you ask me. But don't start any rough stuff. I don't like it. Nor will he. (*She nods and points to the place where she came up*)

BLACK MAN Is he still there? I thought he'd have cut loose and given up long ago. Just you remember that next time I get you alone, I'll . . .

HARLOT That will be fascinating. But we're not alone now, dearie. Look.

(*The third climber appears. He is a bishop, dressed in full bishop's garb*)

BISHOP Well, well, well. Here we all are. Not getting ahead as fast as we hoped, but making good progress on the whole, I think you will agree. Is this the place where we take a rest?

BLACK MAN (*Shouting*) No. No. No rest. We must go faster. We've got to get up there. We dare not waste a moment.

HARLOT A rest. It sounds divine. Just what I need. (*She sits on the ground, and pats the ground beside her, looking up at the Bishop*) Just what all of us need.

BISHOP (*To Black Man*) She may be right, you know. This is not something a man like me can do in a rush. Far better take our time. We don't want to kill ourselves before we get there. (*He sits beside the Harlot*)

BLACK MAN I'll kill you both if you don't hurry. I don't mind killing you. I don't mind killing anybody. I'll kill myself if I must. I don't care about anything except getting to the top.

HARLOT (*To Bishop*) He will kill himself, you know. Look at his face. Look at his bulging muscles. Look at his sweaty sides. He'll drop down any moment if he roars away like that. He'll go pop like a balloon. He'll burst like a bladder. It must be terrible for the blood pressure.

BISHOP Look here, my good man, hadn't you better calm down, sit down and cool down? Let's talk it over like sensible people. No good ever came out of bad temper.

BLACK MAN I'm not in a bad temper. And I'm not your

good man. I'm nobody's man but my own. How long will it be before you white people understand that I belong to *me*? There's no time for mere talking. I'm sick of the sound of it. It's a hissing and a clacking and an emptiness at the end. You've taught me for years that God lives up at the top there. Is it true?

BISHOP True enough, my dear fellow. True enough.

BLACK MAN I'm not your dear fellow. If you call me that once more, bishop or no, I'll tan your hide as well as hers. I'm going to get up there and see God. I've been wanting to talk to Him for a long time. Are you coming with me or not? You said you wanted to see Him, too. Are you going to chicken out now? Or are you coming?

HARLOT What exactly are you going to say to Him?

BLACK MAN I'm going to tell Him I hate Him. I'm going to tell Him that if that's the way He runs the earth, a child could run it better. I'm going to tell Him of centuries of suffering, continents of cruelty, hurt beyond endurance, hate without end, Amen. I'm going to tell Him of beatings, burnings, hunger, disease, torture, misery and chains. And just as we see a glimmer of light, some hope of it becoming a black man's world, the white man with those strong, cunning hands that have grabbed the earth and squeezed it dry for his delight, has made missiles and bombs to blow us all to thunder before we take revenge. (*The Harlot starts laughing*) Are you laughing at me, damn you?

HARLOT Yes. I am. You're so funny. You roar and shout

about "No time for talking", and then do nothing but talk yourself. But will you have the guts to tell God all that? I'd certainly like to be there when you do it. It's almost worth another heave to get to the top.

BLACK MAN Come on. Let's go.

HARLOT I'll let the Bishop decide. We can't leave him alone on the hillside. What do you say, Bishop?

BISHOP It will be quite unsuitable to speak to God in that style. Very wrong indeed. (*To the Black Man*) You'd do far better to talk it over and think about it some more, and even pray about it.

(*The Black Man glares at them both, then suddenly spits on the ground and pulls out a knife. The Harlot shouts "O Lord, he's going to do us in" and hides behind the Bishop. The Bishop looks around and picking up a small piece of rock stands gazing at the Black Man*)

BLACK MAN You've got more guts than I thought, Bishop. But you seem to have forgotten it's Christian to let me hit your cheek, or smash your jaw, or cut your throat without complaint. It's part of Christianity that Christians always forget. If Christianity was like the Christians, the world would have forgotten it long ago. If you try to hit a Christian he sets aside all that nonsense of turning the other cheek and hits you first and hits you hard and keeps on hitting you—especially if you happen to be black. That's why Christian nations have been so good at making wars and empires. No. I'm not going to cut your throats, though both of you deserve it. And never forget, if I cut them, blood would come out the same colour as mine. And it won't be black or white. I'm going to climb up there. I'm going alone. I'm going to have a summit conference with God. That's about it. It's a conference He's not going to forget in a hurry. I'm going to tell Him what I think of Him, what millions of us truly think. I'm going to make Him a fair offer.

BISHOP What offer? It's most irregular to make offers to God without consulting someone like myself.

BLACK MAN You mind your own business.

BISHOP I should say that this emphatically is my business.

BLACK MAN Well, I'm not going to tell you. I've thought it all out. I'm off. (*He turns to the hill*)

HARLOT Suppose you find nothing up there but clouds and mist and the cold winds blowing?

BLACK MAN Then I'll be coming down again with my big shining knife in my big black hand, and I'll be in that bad temper you spoke about, and I'll be looking for you, Bishop.

(*The Black Man turns to the hill, heaves and clambers on to the top tier and vanishes out of sight, going towards the summit. The Bishop and Harlot watch him go*)

HARLOT I hope for your sake he does find something up at the top of the hill. Do you think he will?

BISHOP Certainly he will, my dear. "Seek ye the Lord while He may be found." Isaiah LV, verse 6. "Those that seek me early shall find me." Proverbs VIII, verse 17. All the same, I think it would be a wise precaution to get down to the town again as quickly as possible and tell the police what he said. For his sake, of course, not mine. I wouldn't want him to get into trouble on my account.

HARLOT (*Laughing*) I didn't know bishops were hypocrites.

BISHOP My dear young lady, that's a very improper suggestion.

HARLOT If you think that's an improper suggestion, you should hear some of the suggestions made to me. But you *are* a hypocrite. You were scared when he said that if he found nothing up there, he'd come hunting for you with a knife. If you're so sure he *will* find God, you've nothing to worry about. Why bother to tell the police that he was threatening you?

BISHOP God fulfils Himself in many ways. He might not choose to show Himself to a man full of hate.

HARLOT Come on, Bishop. That won't do for me. I'm a woman full of love. And I've never seen Him.

BISHOP I would not call your kind of love real love.

HARLOT What do you know of my kind of love? You're not supposed to know anything about it. Yet you condemn it.

(*Bishop slowly drops his air of pretence. When he does so, he talks quite differently. He is a humble, rather lost little boy. A human*)

BISHOP Do I?

HARLOT That's better. That's more like the real you talking. Even your voice is different. Tell me something.
Are you like me? Do you spend most of your life
pretending, Bishop? (*Bishop hesitates, then nods*) But
why?

BISHOP Because if men knew what I'm like, they'd stop
believing what I say.

HARLOT But you know what you're like. Have you
stopped believing what you say?

BISHOP Years ago. Years and years and years ago. I don't
know whether I ever really believed it all. That's the
hell of it. It's such a relief to be able to talk to somebody
about it.

HARLOT You can talk to me, Bish. It's fun to find you're
a man after all underneath all those ghastly gaiters.

BISHOP It doesn't seem to matter so much up here on the
hillside, alone with you, with nobody to hear us.

HARLOT Except God Almighty, Bishop. Don't forget
Him. Lord, it is funny, isn't it, to think of me sitting
here on my fanny with a bishop and telling him to
watch his talk in case God's listening in to him.

BISHOP You won't tell anyone what I've said when we
get back?

HARLOT Of course not. I've not got where I have in my
profession without learning to keep confidences. You'd
be surprised the people who come to see me and start
scolding everyone else for their bad ways as soon as
they're out of my sight. Makes them feel better about

their own mess. No. I won't tell on you. If I get tight with the Press boys, mind, I can't promise anything. When I'm tight, I talk. But they never believe anything I say, so you've nothing to worry about really.

BISHOP Sometimes I wish someone would talk, tell everything, so I could throw off my gaiters and my black clothes and go out where nobody knows me and do all the things I've wanted to do and never dared to do— paint, sing, dance, get tight, maybe learn more about your kind of loving.

HARLOT Why don't you? Now's your chance. (*She draws near to him. The Bishop recoils*)

BISHOP Partly fear. Partly that I love being a bishop with everyone bowing and flattering and calling me "My Lord". Even nowadays a lot of people still pay a lot of attention to bishops. But the real thing is . . . (*He hesitates*)

HARLOT Go on. You won't shock me. Have you got a skeleton with a nice covering of warm flesh all over it nestling somewhere in your cupboard?

BISHOP (*Primly*) Certainly not. What an outrageous suggestion. (*Dropping his mask of unreality again*) The truth is that while I do not believe in the things I preach from the pulpit myself, yet for some reason plenty of people say they've found faith through me. It gives them courage. It keeps them happy. It seems somehow terribly important not to let them down. So I just go on pretending.

HARLOT (*Clapping her hands*) Good for you, Bish. It's the first time I've understood a bishop or respected him. That's real love, that is.

BISHOP Is it? Is it love to make people try to live something you think is a lie?

HARLOT Of course it is. It's what I do all the time. Your job and mine seem very much alike, now I come to think of it.

BISHOP (*Laughing in his turn*) I don't see the slightest resemblance.

HARLOT Don't take offence, dearie. You don't get paid half as much as I do. I know that. It's what makes you so much more noble. But the trade of both of us is love, isn't it? God is love, and all that. They used to tell me so at Sunday school when I was a kid. You love 'em enough to fool 'em by giving what you don't like and don't believe in. I'm just the same. The only thing is you seem to keep 'em happy longer than I do.

BISHOP You amaze me. How can you give people your sort of love without liking it?

HARLOT Like it? Do you suppose a girl enjoys being handled and used like a second-hand motor-car on hire with gears being grated by unskilled hands and everyone trying to get the most out of it for the least maintenance? Do you suppose I enjoy sharing my bed with drunks and dotards, teenagers out for a thrill and old men trying to imagine they are still thrillable and thrilling as teenagers? Most people who make love to me are thinking of someone else as they do it. It's true that, like you, I have my regular customers. Some come to me every week, just as others go to your church. But I don't like it any more than you seem to like your job. It's a business. It's the only one I understand. You don't need to know shorthand and typing, to speak foreign languages, to have a university degree, to work as I work. You just need to give the pretence of love without allowing yourself to love anybody.

BISHOP Have you never been in love?

HARLOT I can't afford it. It would ruin me. I have to control my heart as well as my limbs. They just have to do what they are told by me and not what anybody else tells them. I am like a general ordering troops into battle. My body and my heart and my feelings are my troops. I tell them what to do and don't allow them to talk back to me. Or maybe I am like a businessman. My body is like workers in a factory or business. I tell it what to do and it does it. It earns money for me just as workers in industry earn money for the stockholders. But I am my own stockholder. I stand outside the transaction. I don't get involved with my customers. I just give my body the orders and accept the money it brings back to me. I'm making money while my time lasts. When it's all over, perhaps I'll fall in love. But I hope not. It will be too late. Far too late.

BISHOP I wish I'd never told you the truth about myself. I might have been able to give you something that could have helped you.

HARLOT No. That stuff's not for me. I'm glad you told me. I'd never have seen how alike we are if you hadn't. But I'm worried about the Black Man. He won't find anyone on top of that hill, will he?

BISHOP I really don't know. I doubt it. But people in life often find what they are looking for. It'll be interesting to see what happens when he comes down.

HARLOT If he's got a knife in one hand, I'll be interested to see whether or not you run. (*Looking at him*) You wouldn't run, you know. Would you?

BISHOP It's the sort of thing you never know about until it happens. I think I'd probably not run. Imagine what people would say if I did.

HARLOT And think of what they'd say if you didn't.

BISHOP By heavens, we are alike. How did you guess? (*Stands up*) "Modern Martyr Slain by Black Madman." I can just see the headlines. It would be good to be a martyr, even if that was the end of it all. Besides, that man looks as if he knows how to handle a knife. He'd not make a long job of it. Just one sharp pang—then silence, and darkness and the long, blessed sleep. All the same, if he comes with the knife, I expect I'll start running.

HARLOT I hope he finds someone up there. He'll never be happy till he can put his finger on the thing he hates so much. It's like a splinter. You can get it out of your thumb. But unless you see it and look at it and feel it, it's not the same thing. Satisfaction is missing.

BISHOP (*Standing and peering upwards*) He may not get to the top. There's a mist up there. I can't see him.

(*During these last speeches the light has been fading. Darkness is coming*)

HARLOT He'll get there. A man who hates like him will get to the top.

BISHOP He won't get there till dark. We'd better go down.

HARLOT We'll never get down. It's too late. We'd better stay here together. He'll know where to find us.

BISHOP Strange, isn't it? We both have love of one sort or another as our profession. He only hates. He leaves us behind and goes on climbing. There seems more in his hatred than in your sort of love—or mine. There's a sermon in that somewhere.

HARLOT Don't give me a sermon, please. I'm not the type and this is not the place. We're stuck here for the night. We'd better make the best of it. It's not too cold. The ground's not too rough. Come on. (*She pats the earth beside her. The Bishop stands looking at her*) Oh, come on. Don't be so silly. Nobody will see us. (*She pats the ground again*) Come on, I won't hurt you. If we stay close enough together we'll be warm enough. (*He still hesitates*) We can go down in the morning. (*She pats the ground again at her side. The Bishop slowly moves towards her as darkness falls*)

Curtain

SCENE TWO

It is the top of the hill. Mr. Brown sits there reading a paper. It is dazzling light. Mr. Brown's hands are bandaged. He is sitting stage left facing the wings. From stage right, weary, feet dragging behind him, and with a long knife in his hand, comes the Black Man. He stops when he sees Mr. Brown. Then he begins to creep forward.

MR. BROWN (*Without looking round*) I'm glad to see you, my dear fellow. Come and sit down. You must be tired.

BLACK MAN I'm *not* your dear fellow. Don't call me that. I belong to me.

MR. BROWN Splendid. Whatever you say. Certainly I won't call you "my dear fellow" if you don't like it. But, of course, it's exactly what you are.

BLACK MAN Who the hell are you? How did you get up here? What are you doing?

MR. BROWN You've not quite got your bearings yet, have you, after that long climb? I'm reading the newspaper.

BLACK MAN You're nuts. Who would come all the way up here just to read a newspaper?

MR. BROWN A number of people think I'm nuts. Who did you expect to find up here anyway?

BLACK MAN Not you. (*Suddenly a thought hits him. He says slowly*) At least, I don't think it's you. Let's have a look at you. (*Mr. Brown turns round and looks at the Black Man*)

I can't see you very clearly. (*He puts his arms around his eyes*) I can't see anything. I can't see.

MR. BROWN Sorry. It is a bit bright at first, they tell me. Takes a bit of time to get used to it. Somebody once said that character is what you do in the dark. I always think it's how much you can bear to see in the light. I'll take it down a bit for you. (*Mr. Brown lifts up his hand. The lights at once begin to fade. The dazzle dies. Mr. Brown drops his hand again*) There. Is that better?

BLACK MAN (*Removes his arm from his eyes. Looks at Mr. Brown. Rubs his eyes. Looks at Mr. Brown again. Puts away his knife. Speaks very slowly*) I never knew.

MR. BROWN Never knew what?

BLACK MAN Never knew that you were black.

MR. BROWN Am I? So be it, then. As black as ebony. As black as night. As black as pitch in the belly of a cauldron or coal in the bowels of the earth.

BLACK MAN. You're as black as I am.

MR. BROWN If you say so, I'm ready to believe it. Many people tell me many things. I hear them all and believe what I can believe. I'm blind about colour. It doesn't mean much to me. Some say I'm black. For centuries some said I was white. Nowadays some say I'm as yellow as China or as red as Russia. It's odd. Men mostly seem to think I'm the colour that they are themselves.

BLACK MAN You're black all right. It makes a big difference. I don't know what to say to you.

MR. BROWN Why not say what's on your mind? Come on. Sit down. Make yourself comfortable.

BLACK MAN (*Sits*) It's not easy. Not at all easy. Nothing like I thought it would be. (*Noticing the bandages*) Say, have you hurt yourself?

MR. BROWN (*Holding up his hands*) These? Oh, yes. I got them hurt some time ago. They're slow to heal. But don't let that worry you.

BLACK MAN I never thought anyone could hurt you.

MR. BROWN (*Laughing*) Of course they can. I get hurt a lot. Love's unbreakable. But often things snap—and it hurts. Nowadays, you can't love people without getting hurt, and I do love 'em all. The donkeys that worship what's under their hats and between their ears, and the piggies that worship what's below their own belts and inside their pocket-books.

BLACK MAN You can't know what love is. Otherwise you'd stop all this hell on earth.

MR. BROWN You mean all that stuff you were telling your two friends about chains and imperialism and bombs and human butchery?

BLACK MAN How did you hear all that? You were spying on me.

MR. BROWN That's part of my job. I have good ears and my eyes run all over the place while I'm sitting here on the hilltop. I don't stop all that because I don't feel the same way about life or death or pain or justice or colour as you do. Men are free to choose between good and evil, and all have knowledge of it. One day you'll understand things as I do.

BLACK MAN Do stop it. Prove to me you can stop it. Stop the black man's hell on earth. Stop it now. It's gone on too long. It's unbearable. Look. I'll go on my knees to you and beg you to stop it, and that's something I've never done before. (*Does so*) Please, please.

MR. BROWN Very good of you. I appreciate it. Indeed I do. But get up off your knees. Sit down here if you don't mind and let's talk sensibly together. Millions of people every minute of the day go on their knees telling me what they want me to do. I wish I had more who'd sit and listen while I told them what I want them to do. It would save them lives, time, tears, toil and, incidentally, a lot of money from taxation if they had the common sense to do it.

BLACK MAN (*Sitting*) You're hard.

MR. BROWN Did you expect me to be soft? If I'd been soft, you'd have raised even more hell than you have already. Now, what about this offer you are going to make me? You said it's a fair offer. What is it?

BLACK MAN I think you're just a fake.

MR. BROWN That's not an offer. It's an opinion.

BLACK MAN For hundreds of years you've tricked man into believing you made him. I don't believe it.

MR. BROWN That's another opinion. What's the offer?

BLACK MAN I believe you didn't make man but that man made you. I think we made you in our own image because we were too weak, too afraid, too close to the animal to face life and death without you. Now I think we are ready. Man has grown up. He can in the next generation or so destroy the God he made. We can do without Him.

MR. BROWN Go ahead and try. It's not the first time it's been attempted, you know.

BLACK MAN It's the first time for hundreds of years that the whole world is turning against Him.

MR. BROWN There's more people on His side than you guess. The trouble is they're too lazy and too comfortable and too compromising. But when things get rougher they'll start to live straight and work together, you'll see. A few more Stalins, a few more Hitlers, a few more martyrdoms. Then they'll wake up.

BLACK MAN How can you dare to talk like that?

MR. BROWN It's not a matter of daring. It's a matter of caring. I just don't think as you think, nor act as you act. I never have and never will. I've a different set of values. Sometimes men decide to make their own hells on earth before they turn their hearts to heaven. It's as wicked and foolish as people who gash themselves with knives so as to enjoy it when they stop. By the way, if man made me in his own image, why do you think I look at everything so differently from man? It's funny you didn't make me more like you when you had the chance.

BLACK MAN I don't believe in you.

MR. BROWN You do, you know. That's what makes you

so cross. If you didn't believe in me, I wouldn't worry you so much. Nobody gets so worked up trying to destroy something they think isn't really there. You could do all sorts of things you'd like to do if deep down you didn't believe in me. The trouble with all you No-Godders is that you think you are little gods yourselves. It's Jehovah Great You Are. And you know if that's true there's no hope for humanity. Every man who thinks at all, however noisy and violent his worship of the No-God, in the silences of the night and the solitude of his heart feels himself not alone but in some relation to the universe.

BLACK MAN I don't understand that.

MR. BROWN Never mind. The point is that you can't make what you call a fair offer to someone you don't believe in.

BLACK MAN My offer is this. Come back down the hill with me. You can't expect everyone to get up here. They don't hate you as much as I do. Or rather as much as I did.

MR. BROWN Hating a bit less, are you? That's good.

BLACK MAN It's bad.

MR. BROWN You think you'll get your way by hating. You are wrong.

BLACK MAN How else will I get it?

MR. BROWN By loving.

BLACK MAN Loving? Loving those swine who sneer and beat and bully and kill?

MR. BROWN   Yes. Nothing else will touch them. It's what they need. And it's what you want. You want a load of it. You want men to love you because of your black skin. But you hate them because of their black hearts. Hate has a million children. It breeds in every climate all the time. What others do to you and your people makes you hate more and more and more. You are run by it. It blinds you. It binds you. It drags you down to the dust and holds you there bleeding and grovelling. It is your dictator. You become the slave of hate, so you become the slave of the men who cause the hatred, which is the last thing you want, and nothing changes.

BLACK MAN   I'll say it changes. We're going up, not down. We're winning. We'll be free.

MR. BROWN   Not really free. Hate will still be there with its dictatorship. And it will soon end your freedom with new dictatorships. It's like acid. It eats away the walls of the heart that contains it. Soon you will start hating men who are not white. There's no birth-control in hate. It breeds and multiplies, even in the family circle. No. Hate what they do by all means. But love what they can become and help them to become it. With their poisoned personalities and wicked hands they need as much love as you, poor devils. You are a big enough man to give to them.

BLACK MAN   I am not. I don't want any of it. It's impossible.

MR. BROWN   Impossible? You came along saying you

hated me. But you told me you hated me less just now.

BLACK MAN I don't know. I'm not sure. You make things so difficult. You're black.

MR. BROWN (*Laughing*) You make things so easy. It's as silly to love somebody just because you think their skin is black as to hate somebody just because you think their blood is blue. Why do you want me to come with you?

BLACK MAN I want you to confront humanity with all its modern knowhow. I want you to have a dialogue with them. I want to see if you have the guts to stand up to it, or whether you'll just be argued into dust by the beatnik bishops and sexy satirists, by the pious frauds and perverted theologians. I want you to prove yourself.

MR. BROWN To whom?

BLACK MAN To everybody.

MR. BROWN You mean to prove myself to you, don't you?

BLACK MAN No. I don't. I'm thinking of that bishop and the girl on the hillside. I suppose they're still on the hillside?

MR. BROWN They're still there. They'll be waiting for us.

BLACK MAN Us? Does that mean you're coming?

MR. BROWN I guessed what you were going to suggest to me. It's a job I don't much like. But I think you may be right. It may be the best way to settle this argument.

BLACK MAN When shall we go?

MR. BROWN As soon as you're ready.

BLACK MAN Let's go. Let's go now. (*He turns and strides off, then stops*) By the way, there's one thing that bothers me.

MR. BROWN Only one thing? What's that?

BLACK MAN What would you like me to call you? When we are down there, I mean?

MR. BROWN Doesn't bother me at all. It's not of the smallest consequence. Call me anything you like. One name's as good as another to me. I've been called most things in my time.

BLACK MAN You choose. You see, I can't very well introduce you to people as—well, what you really are. Or what you say you are.

MR. BROWN I don't think I've said I'm anything, have I?

BLACK MAN You know what I mean.

MR. BROWN Yes. I know.

BLACK MAN It had better be something simple, something easy to remember.

MR. BROWN That would be a help.

BLACK MAN What do they call you around here?

MR. BROWN They don't really need to call me anything. We know each other pretty well. And the names they have called me from time to time would not be right now.

BLACK MAN I can't think of a name. You suggest one.

MR. BROWN How about Mr. White?

BLACK MAN No, by God, anything but that.

MR. BROWN (*Laughs*) Sorry. I was only teasing you.
I need a sense of humour, you know, and sometimes
folk think it runs away with me. If I didn't know how
to laugh I'd spend my days in crying. Well, what about
Mr. Brown?

BLACK MAN Mr. Brown? All right. It suits me if it suits
you. I'll dig that. You lead the way. Let's go. After
you, Mr. Brown.

MR. BROWN No. After you. You know where your
friends are waiting.

BLACK MAN Meaning you don't? Very well. Come on,
Mr. Brown. Down the hill we go.

(*The Black Man leads Mr. Brown out as the scene ends*)

Curtain

SCENE THREE

*We are back once more on the hillside. Dawn is breaking.
The Bishop and the Harlot are stretched side by side asleep on
the ground. Suddenly the Harlot sits up. She listens. Then
she begins to make up her face.*

HARLOT Hey, Bishop. Wake up. (*The Bishop does not
move. After looking at him, she shouts again and louder*)
Wakey, wakey, Bish. You'd better hurry. Somebody's

coming. (*No sign nor sound from the Bishop. The Harlot stands up and shakes him awake. The Bishop comes to life with a grunt and a groan*) You may be a bishop, but you're as hard to waken as a drunken sailor on a Sunday morning.

BISHOP (*Stretching his arms*) I live in a palace. My bed is as soft as wool and sweet as honey. I have servants to tuck me in at night and turn me out at morning. I lie in it through dark hours and my heart is like a sword inside me. I pray for the morning. But in this wild place with a stone in the small of my back, damp from the earth that will give me pains for weeks, ants crawling up and down inside my gaiters (*He stands and scratches vigorously*), I've slept better than I have for years. I begin to remember what it was like to feel young and hopeful and happy. It must be your influence.

HARLOT I slept well myself. My bed at home's not like yours. It's restful to spend a night under the stars without anyone to trouble me. (*She listens*) There's somebody coming. I can hear them scrambling on the rocks.

BISHOP Coming up or coming down?

HARLOT Down.

(*Bishop brushes down his clothes, smooths his hair*)

BISHOP (*Urgently*) I want you to promise me something. Before too long let's meet sometime, anywhere, and talk again. There are so many things I want to hear from you and tell you.

HARLOT Be your age, Bishop. Don't talk foolishness. Of course we mustn't meet again. I'd like to oblige you, mind. But I daren't do it. You might be able to afford it. You might get away with it. But it would ruin me. Professionally, I mean. I just can't afford to have a friendship with a man in your position. My clients wouldn't understand it. And they wouldn't like it. No, dearie. No more of this for you and me.

BISHOP You're right, my dear young lady. Of course you are right. Your unselfishness does you credit.

HARLOT It's not unselfish. It's selfish. I've got to look after myself. You can't have the wrong sort of friends in my work. People stay away if you are suspected of respectability. Snobbish in a funny sort of inside-out, upside-down style. But there it is.

(*The Black Man appears on the top tier of the hill*)

BLACK MAN Hello. Are you all right?

HARLOT Yes. We're fine. (*To Bishop*) I was waiting to see whether you'd run if he had a knife in his big black hand. Remember? But I don't see any knife.

BISHOP And I don't see anyone with him. (*To Black Man*) Thank God you are safe, my friend. I have been praying for you all night long.

HARLOT (*Giggling*) Yes. So have I. We've been praying *together*. Haven't we, Bishop?

BLACK MAN You'd better do some more praying. You'd better make it good.

HARLOT What do you mean?

BLACK MAN I've got a friend with me. He's called Mr. Brown. He's just behind me. But I want to warn you not to be amazed when you see him.

BISHOP What should amaze us?

BLACK MAN He's black.

HARLOT There's nothing amazing in that. The world's full of people of different colours. I can tell you one thing. The colour of a man's skin doesn't settle anything. It's what's inside the skin that counts.

(*Black Man climbs down from top to middle tier. Shouts back*)

BLACK MAN Come on, Mr. Brown. (*Mr. Brown appears on top tier*)

MR. BROWN Good morning. I'm glad to see you both. And glad you slept well.

HARLOT How did you know we slept well?

BLACK MAN He's got long ears. Sound carries far on this hillside. I could hear you both saying something about sleep myself as I came down the rocks.

BISHOP (*To Harlot*) Do you think he's gone out of his mind? The height has affected him or something. That person with him is no more black than a polar bear. He's as white as you or I.

HARLOT Don't talk so loud. You'll only upset somebody. And it's not worth it. Why make a fuss? If he thinks the man's black, let him be black. Why bother? He may know him better than we do. You'd be surprised how many people are different from what they seem or what they say when you see them in their birthday suit.

BISHOP My dear young lady, I hope you will spare us that sort of vulgarity at this hour of the day. Or any hour, come to that. It's unnecessary.

HARLOT Have it your own way, Bishop. Any hour of day or night is all the same to me.

BLACK MAN We'd better be getting down the hill.

BISHOP Yes. The sooner we get back to normal, the better.

HARLOT Haven't you forgotten something, Bishop?

BISHOP What do you mean?

HARLOT I don't know much about bishops. But I always thought they started the day with Bibles and prayers and blessings and what not. You haven't got a Bible here. It would be a heavy old thing to take up a hill like this. But I've been with you all night long and you've said no prayers. You've said no blessings. Nothing. It's none of my business, of course, but I like to see things done right.

BLACK MAN I thought you were both praying for me all night long.

BISHOP Exactly. Silent prayer, as you might say. Silent prayer.

(*Mr. Brown kneels down*)

BLACK MAN What are you on your knees for?

MR. BROWN I imagined the Bishop would want to accept the young lady's suggestion. It seemed to me a good idea.

(*They look at each other. Then the Harlot starts to giggle.*

She kneels.   The Black Man kneels.   The Bishop stands saying nothing.   There is a long pause.   Then Mr. Brown stands up)

HARLOT   Is that all? Have we finished?

BISHOP   Yes.

BLACK MAN   A silent blessing, as you might say.   A silent blessing.

MR. BROWN   I often think they are best, don't you?   So many people use their ears but never their brains when they are being blessed.   They let the blesser do the work while they do nothing.

BLACK MAN   It's no blessing to have to work.

MR. BROWN   It's a blessing to start giving something to other people.

BLACK MAN   Why?

MR. BROWN   Good people, or people who think they are good, treat a blesser like a cow.   They just want to milk him dry.   It's bad for them.   It's a curse not a blessing.

BISHOP   (*To Mr. Brown*) If you could come down I'd like a word in your ear.   A private word.

(Mr. Brown makes no reply, but at once comes down on to the middle tier and on to the lower tier.)

BISHOP   Thank you for what you said.   I see you understand blessings and bishops.   Now, I want to say something to you.   It's about the girl.

MR. BROWN   Oh, very well.

BISHOP   You sound surprised.

MR. BROWN A little. Yes. I thought from the way you asked me to come down and talk with you that the first person you might wish to speak about was yourself.

BISHOP In my profession, Mr. Brown, or rather my calling, I have to learn never to put myself first.

MR. BROWN That must be difficult.

BISHOP Not really. It becomes almost a habit after a time. Anyway, I want you to understand the girl. She's well-meaning, I'm sure. Good-hearted. But—well, I don't quite know how to express it.

MR. BROWN Just say what you mean.

BISHOP I don't want to shock you. You see, I have to tackle so many ugly things in life. The modern world is full of machinery, newspapers, television shows, science, traffic, luxury. We're a sophisticated generation. It's—well—it's . . .

MR. BROWN What you're trying to say is that things have changed since I was last here, and you can't expect me to understand modern society?

BISHOP Exactly.

MR. BROWN I understand enough, if it's really the girl you want to talk about, to know that she's a whore.

BISHOP Mr. Brown, that's not the way I like to hear any woman spoken about.

MR. BROWN Why not? A whore's a whore, just as a fraud is a fraud. In your profession the body is supposed to be of less importance than the soul. Why then do you make such a fuss about sex and sickness and hunger and

M.B.—D

war, but think little or nothing of souls stinking with bitterness, communities sour with hate of class and race, nations dying from disobedience?

BISHOP I don't want to get into any sort of argument with you.

MR. BROWN I'm not arguing.

BISHOP All I want to say is, please do not judge the girl too harshly. She is what others made her.

MR. BROWN Nonsense. She is what she made herself. You'll never help her if you let her think it's all someone else's fault. That's the trouble with you moderns. You always try to make excuses for people by blaming environment or education or some such thing. It's the result of years of excusing yourselves.

BISHOP You're hard.

MR. BROWN Am I? Now, why don't you stop all this and say what's really troubling you?

BISHOP You may find she's a liar.

MR. BROWN Whores often are. They have to be.

BISHOP I wouldn't want you to believe everything she said.

MR. BROWN About you?

BISHOP Not exactly. But after a night out here together a woman might imagine all manner of things.

MR. BROWN I'll not heed her imaginings.

BISHOP Good. I'm grateful. Now I think we'd better be on our way down the hill. I want you to meet my fellow clergy, Mr. Brown. I want you to meet all manner of men. I mean to do my very best to help you understand the world we're living in. It's changing fast. Things aren't going quite so well as we'd choose. But we're making progress. Oh, yes. I think we can say without risk of boasting that we are making progress.

(*The Bishop climbs out of sight down the hill. Mr. Brown watches him go. The Harlot comes to him*)

HARLOT Gone on ahead, has he? Not a bad old stick. I want a word with you about him.

MR. BROWN Yes. He was afraid you would.

HARLOT He's scared to death. I know that. A night out on a hillside with a girl like me. What will everybody say? What do you say, Mr. Brown?

MR. BROWN I say that nothing happened except in his heart—and yours.

HARLOT If everybody believed that, I'd be ruined. People would think I'm losing my grip. Don't tell anyone, will you, Mr. Brown?

MR. BROWN No. Of course not. But I tell you that what happens in someone's heart is as important as what may happen in their bed—or in somebody else's.

HARLOT Now look here, dearie . . . Oh, Lord, I suppose I shouldn't call you "dearie", should I?

MR. BROWN Why not?

HARLOT Well, if you don't mind it, there's no reason why I should. Don't be too rough with him, dearie. He hasn't had the advantages a girl like me has had. He's had everything on the cheap. He knows so little about people. He can't help being what he is.

MR. BROWN That's what he said about you.

HARLOT Did he, indeed? What impudence. I'm what I make myself.

MR. BROWN I told him that. He got angry. Then he offered to show me around the modern world.

HARLOT He couldn't tell you or me anything. He's all tied up and doesn't know it. He's so full of himself he doesn't know what's going on around him. But he was decent to me. Real decent. I don't want you to be hard on him. Be nice to him—for my sake.

MR. BROWN He said I was hard.

HARLOT Well, don't be, dearie. It doesn't suit you.

MR. BROWN And this sort of thing doesn't suit you, either.

HARLOT What sort of thing?

MR. BROWN This constant pretending to be what you're not.

HARLOT I'd be lost if I stopped pretending. Pretence is my shield. I'd get hurt all day long if I stopped pretending.

MR. BROWN You look lovely when you are being yourself.

HARLOT My boyfriends say they love me best when I am pretending to be what they want.

MR. BROWN They lie.

HARLOT We all lie.

MR. BROWN I don't. I tell you straight, this has got to stop.

HARLOT What's got to stop?

MR. BROWN You know very well what you've known for a long time. There's to be no more of it. Never again. Understand? If I'm to treat that bishop well for your sake, you must treat yourself well—for mine.

HARLOT Mind your own business.

MR. BROWN This is my business.

HARLOT Who'd look after me if I stopped? It's the only way I know to get along.

MR. BROWN I'd look after you.

HARLOT Is that a proposition?

MR. BROWN (*After looking at her for a while*) Yes. It is. In a sense, it is. I'm going down the hill now. I'll be seeing you. (*He goes. The Black Man comes towards the Harlot*)

BLACK MAN What were you talking about with him?

HARLOT Nothing much. The Bishop mostly.

BLACK MAN I'm not sure he and the Bishop get along too well. What do you think?

HARLOT I think your Mr. Brown's rather ducky.

BLACK MAN He'd better watch his step. He'll be a dead ducky if he's not careful.

HARLOT You'd better look after him. I'm not sure if he can look after himself.

BLACK MAN I'll try.

(*They go down as the curtain falls*)

Curtain

SCENE FOUR

We see a bar frequented by pressmen. Behind the bar the Harlot is serving drinks. Some pressmen and women are reading newspapers, talking, drinking. One pressman is half-tight. He is called Andy.

ANDY Fill it up with Scotch, dear.

HARLOT You'rve had enough, Andy.

ANDY Shut up. You're not here to preach. Give me a bottle.

(*He dives across the bar, grabs one of the bottles, pours himself a drink, drains it, fills his glass again and keeps hold of the bottle*)

DOCTOR She's right, you know, Andy.

ANDY You shut up, too. I thought you were my friend.

DOCTOR I'm your doctor.

ANDY Yes. And don't forget I pay you fees to keep me healthy doing what I want, not to make me miserable trying to stop me doing what you don't want. I say, that doesn't sound quite right, does it? (*He drinks again and refills his glass from the bottle*)

DOCTOR As a doctor, seriously I tell you you ought to stop. You'll drop dead one day if you go on like this. As a friend I tell you, you'll upset her. (*Pointing at the Harlot*) She's looking good these days, too.

ANDY That's right. So she is. (*He grabs the Harlot's arm across the bar*) You're looking beautiful, my dear. Lovely. Gorgeous. Delectable. Ravishing. Come on, fellows, help me out. Think of a few more words for me.

FIRST PRESSMAN Delicious!

SECOND PRESSMAN Seductive!

PRESSWOMAN Maddening!

ANDY That's it. Maddening. She maddens me. (*To Harlot*) You look younger, darling. Lots and lots and lots younger. How do you do it? (*He pulls her half across the bar to him and tries to kiss her*)

HARLOT Let me go and I'll tell you.

ANDY (*Letting go*) Very well. Tell. Tell us the secret of eternal youth.

HARLOT You're crazy. If you want the secret, I'll tell you. Every whisky you swallow takes ten years off my life so far as you are concerned.

ANDY She's a wise girl. She's absolutely right, you know. Absolutely right. Hey, the bottle's empty. (*He holds it upside down*) Give me another bottle and I'll have you back in the cradle before you know what's become of you.

(*Harlot gives him another bottle and swiftly moves away before Andy can grab her arm again*)

(*Peering at her*) Something has happened to her. I wouldn't have recognised her. She *does* look younger.

DOCTOR If you don't sober up, you won't have the chance of looking at her any more. She's fed up with you, Andy. She'll drop you.

ANDY Drop me? She can't afford to drop me. She can no more drop me than I can drop the drink. And why not? Because I'm good for her, just as the drink is good for me. We're like two blades to a pair of scissors. We're like two legs to a pair of trousers. We're inseparable. Aren't we, darling?

(*Enter the Black Man*)

BLACK MAN Andy! Andy! I'm so glad to see you. I've been looking for you all over town.

ANDY Well, here I am, fellow, here I am. Siddown. Have a drink.

BLACK MAN No. Not now. Andy, there's something important I've got to tell you. Come over here. I want to talk.

(*He drags Andy downstage, where they sit on two stools, Andy still clutching his bottle. The Doctor and other pressmen go on talking together around the bar*)

Andy, are you all right?

ANDY 'Course I'm all right.

BLACK MAN Are you sober?

ANDY Sober enough.

BLACK MAN Sober enough to do something for me?

ANDY Never let you down yet, have I, fellow? What
is it?

BLACK MAN You're the best friend I've got. You've stuck
to me when everything seemed against me. I reckon if
every white man dipped his pen in the inkpot you use,
there'd be less blood spilt around the earth. You've got
guts. You say what you think in print as well as in
private.

ANDY (*Clapping Black Man on the back*) Tolerance,
fellow, tolerance. That's the secret. Brothers under the
skin and all that and all that. I just can't bear folk who
exploit and despise and use other people. Down with
imperialism and up with brotherhood. That's all I say.

BLACK MAN I need your help. I need it badly.

ANDY What is it, fellow?

BLACK MAN There's a man I met. He's coming here soon.
He's called Brown. He says he's a friend of my people,
Andy. But I'm not sure. I'm not quite sure. I want you
to find out for me. You've investigated more rackets,
you've exposed more frauds than any other pressman
I know. It's important for me to know whether this
man is on the level. It's important for us all.

ANDY Do you think he's on the level or don't you?

BLACK MAN I'd like to think he is. But somehow I can't.

ANDY Leave him to me, fellow. Just leave him to me.
I can see through a crook in no time.

BLACK MAN Even when . . .? (*He points to the bottle still
clutched in Andy's hand*)

ANDY Especially when. Say, what's this guy done to you?

BLACK MAN Something terrible. He made me doubt my hate. And it's all I've got to go on.

ANDY (*Holding out the bottle to him*) Have a drink, fellow. Have a drink.

BLACK MAN (*Paying no heed*) He said hate wouldn't work.

ANDY What would?

BLACK MAN Love.

ANDY (*Starting to laugh*) Don't fall for that stuff. Love's fun—but it creates more problems than it cures. Look at us. All of us problems. And all of us caused by love. White men, black men, yellow men, brown men, everybody's doing it. And where are we?

BLACK MAN He didn't mean that sort of love.

ANDY The only sort I know.

BLACK MAN That's not true, Andy. You've shown me love, even when I've been drunk and difficult and dangerous. Yes. (*He stands up*) By God, yes. He meant the sort of love we all of us need and few of us give. He seemed to think it dangerous that hate is fiercer than love in the world. And that it's everybody's fault and not just the white man's which makes it so.

ANDY Sit down, fellow. Take it easy. Don't let him rattle you. I'd like to meet this Mr. Brown of yours. People like that don't understand anything about any-thing. They want to stop us smoking, gambling, whoring, laughing and hating too. They want to turn life into greyness. Their love is pale, sickly, above all dull. It's coward-yellow, not blood-red. You are right to hate. It's the only manly thing to do. The trouble with you is that you don't hate enough, and you don't drink enough either. That's something else your Mr. Brown will want to stop, I suppose. Here. Have another. (*Holds the bottle up to the light*) And it's empty. Time to fill up with gas. Come along, fellow. (*He drags the Black Man to the bar. He bangs on it. He shouts*) Hey! My little maddener. Whisky! Give me more whisky!

HARLOT (*From other end of the bar, where she is serving someone else*) You've had enough. I won't give you more, dearie. Honest, it's better I don't.

ANDY If you won't give me more, I'll come over and get it myself, and get you, too. (*He starts to scramble over the bar. The Black Man holds him back*)

BLACK MAN Take it easy, Andy. Take it easy.

HARLOT Stop him, somebody. There'll only be trouble. Doctor, can't you tell him to stop?

DOCTOR I've told him. I keep on telling him. But I'll tell him again. (*He goes over to Andy*) Andy, you've had enough. You've had more than enough. If you go on like this, you won't need me any more.

ANDY What did I tell you? It's the best medicine that ever came out of any bottle. You may know most insides, Doctor, but you don't know mine. Whisky's the cure for chilblains, ulcers, pox, ringworm and tape-worm so far as my gut goes. (*To Harlot*) Did you hear what he said, darling? He said if I had another bottle of

Scotch, I'd be cured of everything and never need a doctor again. It's the doctor saying it.

DOCTOR You won't need this doctor or any doctor. You'll just be lying quiet in your last suit with your hands folded on your chest, your toes turned to heaven and your soul already there—I hope.

SECOND PRESSMAN I doubt.

DOCTOR It's not so much the Scotch whisky as the Irish temper. When you drink, you fight. When you fight, your pressure goes up like a helicopter. You'll do it once too often and down you'll drop like a lead balloon. You'll never get up again. You'll be a goner.

ANDY (*With a sudden furious double leap, thrusting the Black Man and the Doctor aside and leaping on to the bar*) Here I am, up like a helicopter. To hell with you, Doctor. To hell with the lot of you. You don't know what you're talking about. (*To the Harlot*) And here I come, darling, down like a lead balloon to get that bottle— and to get you, too. (*He jumps down on the other side of the bar. The Harlot has snatched up the bottle. She runs as far as she can from him*)

HARLOT Keep off me. Keep him off me. You shan't. Leave me alone. You're drunk.

ANDY (*Wrestling to get the bottle, and to grab her and kiss her. They struggle as they shout at each other*) Yes, I'm drunk. Drunk with your loveliness, my little maddener.

HARLOT I'm not your maddener.

ANDY Oh yes, you are.

HARLOT I don't belong to you or any man.

ANDY Oh yes, you do.

HARLOT You'll smash everything, you fool.

(*In the midst of this fight, with glass and bottles crashing behind the bar, the Pressmen, the Black Man, the Doctor look on laughing, roaring words of encouragement or discouragement according to their mood*)

FIRST PRESSMAN Hit him, honey. My money's on the girl.

BLACK MAN Be careful, Andy.

SECOND PRESSMAN Which'll he get, bottle or girl?

DOCTOR Both.

PRESSWOMAN You men are all alike. Disgusting.

FIRST PRESSMAN You can't stop watching it, can you, dear?

SECOND PRESSMAN It's a long time since anyone treated you that way.

(*The Harlot by now is backed against the wall. Andy has her round the waist and is forcing her to kiss him. She still holds the bottle high and away from him*)

HARLOT (*Shouting*) Help me, someone. Cowards. Cowards.

(*Mr. Brown comes in as she is shouting. He walks straight into the middle of it all*)

MR. BROWN Certainly, I'll help you.

(*All turn and look at him*)

ANDY (*Mockingly*) You—help her? And who may you be? Hercules?

(*They all laugh except the Black Man*)

BLACK MAN This is Mr. Brown, Andy. You remember I spoke to you about him.

ANDY So he's your Mr. Brown, is he? It'll be interesting to see how he'll help.

MR. BROWN (*To the Harlot*) I'd give him the bottle if I were you. (*She hesitates, annoyed*) All right. Give it to me. It's probably better so. If you'll all sit down, I'll give you all a drink.

ANDY Well, what do you know? Service with a smile. He may be a help if he goes on like this. A real help. Very well. Give him the bottle, dear. You heard him. (*He comes out from behind the bar, sits down with the Black Man. He does not take his eyes off Mr. Brown. The Harlot in wonder gives Mr. Brown the bottle. It is new. He opens it. The Harlot goes and gives everyone new glasses, with siphons of soda*)

HARLOT (*To Andy*) Calm down, dearie. There's a good man. I hope I didn't hurt you.

ANDY (*Trying to snatch at her arm, but she pushes him away*) Only my heart, darling. Only my heart.

(*Mr. Brown comes to Andy first, but he makes a sweeping gesture*)

Others first, Mr. Brown. The first shall be last. Give 'em all a drink and I'll finish the bottle.

(*Mr. Brown goes quietly round filling the glasses and helping people to soda or water as they decide. When he comes to Andy he pours from the bottle and stops*)

More.

(*Mr. Brown pours again*)

More.

(*Mr. Brown pours again. Andy grabs the bottle from him, fills the glass, jumps up and shouts a toast*)

Here's to Mr. Brown, bouncers' companion, saviour of helpless women, a very present help in trouble.

(*All cheer and drink the toast to Mr. Brown*)

(*Letting out a roar*) What's wrong with my drink? It's poisoned. I've never tasted anything like it. (*He takes another gulp, then spits it on the floor*) By God. It's a trick. It's water. I'd almost forgotten the taste of it, but I remember now. It's water.

(*The Black Man, who has drained his own glass, picks up the bottle from beside Andy, pours himself a drink, looking all the time at Mr. Brown, and tastes it*)

BLACK MAN It's whisky, Andy. Good whisky, too.

(*Andy empties his glass into the ashtray, tips another noggin from the bottle, tastes it, spits it out again*)

ANDY It's water, I tell you. It's a conspiracy. You're all in it.

DOCTOR He's drunk. He wouldn't know the taste of anything.

ANDY I'm *not* drunk. And if I were as drunk as Falstaff I'd still know what whisky tastes like.

(*Second Pressman goes across. Helps himself to the bottle*

while all watch him. Drinks. Nods to Mr. Brown and goes back to his table)

SECOND PRESSMAN If that's water, every tap in town will have a queue at it. It's whisky all right.

FIRST PRESSMAN Andy's tight.

SECOND PRESSMAN Come to think of it, that's probably the explanation of the old water into wine stuff. They were all so tight they didn't know what they were drinking.

ANDY I'm not tight. It's a trick. (*Going over to Mr. Brown, who stands quite still, looking at him*) And you're the one who played it.

MR. BROWN I'd be careful.

ANDY Are you threatening me? (*Takes Mr. Brown by the shoulder and shakes him fiercely*)

MR. BROWN (*When he has finished*) No. Just warning you.

BLACK MAN (*Coming across to Andy*) Come on now. Sit down. There's been enough trouble already.

ANDY (*Dropping his hands from Mr. Brown's shoulders*) Whose side are you on? I've stood up for you and your crowd long enough. I thought you'd stand up for me. What's he done for you, anyway? What's he done for any of us except trick me into drinking water for the first time in years? You asked me to see whether he's a friend or not. Well, I can tell you he is not. I know his sort. I'll bet he's the sort of soft, silly, sentimental, do-gooder who preaches away but won't take a stand on anything that counts. (*To Mr. Brown*) What do you

think of segregation and apartheid and all that hellish-
ness?

MR. BROWN I think a man who exploits and bullies a
woman because her body is different from his own
hasn't much he can say to a man who bullies and exploits someone because he is a different colour.

ANDY What exactly do you mean by that?

MR. BROWN Bedroom or bar-room imperialism is no
better and no worse than the imperialists men like you
make such a howl about. A man who wants to force
another person's body for his pleasure is in much the
same mood as someone who wants to force another
person's sweat and skill for his purse—and just as selfish.

ANDY (*Speaking slowly*) You filthy man. I wouldn't talk
that way if I'd drunk all the whisky in town—especially
in the presence of ladies. But I'm beginning to understand you. I'm beginning to get your shape and size,
Mr. Brown. You're one of these pious puritans who
stick their nose into other people's business without
being asked and make disgusting suggestions that should
never be made. You're against drink and you're against
sex, it seems.

DOCTOR For heaven's sake, Andy, take it easy.

MR. BROWN I'm for what's right and against what's
wrong.

ANDY Wrong? Right? Who's to decide?

MR. BROWN Something inside each one of us will tell.
Sex and drink and you and I all exist. We're all here.
M.B.—E

I face things as they are. That's all. And it's time you
faced them. You'll have to face them.

ANDY (*Seizes his shoulders again, shaking them to emphasise
each point, and becoming more and more excited as he goes
on*) I'm facing you. I'm not a bit afraid of you. I know
the kind of person you are.

MR. BROWN Do you?

ANDY Yes, I do. You persecute people in the name of
God. I suppose you denounce and hound down anyone
who isn't what you call moral? You're a McCarthy of
morality. You're a witch hunter of whores and pimps.
You're intolerant. You've no charity, damn you. None
at all.

MR. BROWN I haven't denounced or hounded down anyone here. If you're talking about sex, I won't pretend
to tolerate the intolerable.

ANDY What do you mean by that, you hypocrite?

MR. BROWN The most uncharitable thing on earth is to
pretend sin is not sin, and that it needs no cure, that
there's no cure for it. That's cruel and loveless. That's
the sin against the Holy Ghost.

ANDY To hell with you and your ghosts. You're a dictator.
That's what you are. If a person doesn't hurt other
people, he should decide for himself what's best. But
you come poking your dirty nose into everybody's
business, smelling filth where there's no filth. You're
a sexual fascist. That's what you are.

MR. BROWN Be careful, Andy.

ANDY (*Shaking Mr. Brown, his voice getting louder and faster and more excited as he goes on*) I won't be careful. Everybody knows that there are some things that can't be cured. It's a mocking of God to pretend they can be. If God could cure, He would. If God can cure and doesn't, then His name is not love. It is hate. He must hate men and I hate Him. I hate Him. I tell you, I hate Him.

(*Andy lets go of Mr. Brown, clutches his throat, gives a terrible cry and falls on the ground. Everybody stands up and rushes forward. The Doctor kneels down crying,* "Stand back. Stand back, please." *He examines him rapidly, undoes his collar, feels his pulse, listens to his heart.*)

DOCTOR Call an ambulance. We must get him out of here. (*As Second Pressman goes to telephone, he shouts after him*) Better call the police, too. (*He stands up*) Bring him into the sitting-room. There's a couch there.

(*They carry him out. The Black Man and the Harlot are left with Mr. Brown*)

HARLOT Is he—is he dead, do you think?

MR. BROWN Better ask the doctor, he'll tell you.

HARLOT You did it.

MR. BROWN I did nothing except give him the bottle he asked for and the answer he desired.

HARLOT Poor devil. Poor old Andy. He treated me like dirt when the drink was on him. But there was goodness in him, too, after his fashion.

MR. BROWN I'm glad to hear you say so. I agree.

BLACK MAN You hated him.

MR. BROWN You do not understand hate or love.

BLACK MAN Hate is stronger than love. I hate you.

MR. BROWN Love is stronger than hate. And I love you, just as I love him—and her. (*Points to the Harlot*)

BLACK MAN We'll soon see which is stronger. Take that!

(*He goes up to Mr. Brown and punches him in the face. Mr. Brown says nothing for a moment. He stands looking at the Black Man. Then he lifts his bandaged hands towards the Black Man. Blood is coming through the bandages*)

You're bleeding.

(*Mr. Brown looks at his hands and nods*)

MR. BROWN So I am.

BLACK MAN I didn't do that. I didn't touch your hands. Tell me I didn't do it.

MR. BROWN They bleed quite often. It's an old wound that takes a long time to heal. Don't blame yourself too much for it.

BLACK MAN I'll never stop blaming myself. Never. Never. Keep away from me. Keep away. Don't come near me. (*He is backing towards the door. Mr. Brown's arms are stretched out to him. But he goes*)

HARLOT Are you afraid of him?

MR. BROWN (*Smiling*) He seemes to be afraid of me.

HARLOT He hit you. You didn't hit him back.

MR. BROWN I didn't need to hit him.

HARLOT I thought he'd fall down like Andy. Why did you let this one hit you and do nothing—while poor old Andy . . . (*She hides her face in her hands and begins to sob*)

MR. BROWN Don't go imagining things. It won't help anybody. You find in life people get the treatment they understand. And what happened tonight is about the only thing Andy would understand—or the Black Man. Some folk have to be hurt. Some have to realise how they have hurt other people.

HARLOT Which kind am I?

MR. BROWN You're the kind that just needs to start life all over again.

HARLOT You're joking.

MR. BROWN I'm not.

HARLOT I'd need help.

MR. BROWN I'll help you.

HARLOT (*Slowly*) Did you mean what you said just now?

MR. BROWN About love?

HARLOT You said you loved me.

MR. BROWN I do.

HARLOT You know, for the first time in my life I'm not afraid to fall in love myself. I think it would be safe to love you.

MR. BROWN Not a bit of it. The most dangerous thing you could possibly do. And far the wisest. (*He moves towards the door*)

HARLOT Are you going?

MR. BROWN I must. Your friend, the Bishop, wants me.
He's waiting.

HARLOT Can I come with you?

MR. BROWN No. You stay here. The police will come.
They'll want to know where I am.

HARLOT Don't worry, dearie. I won't tell 'em. I never
tell 'em a thing.

MR. BROWN But you must. Tell them where they can
find me. They'll need to know. (*He goes*)

HARLOT He loves me. (*She dances a few steps for joy*) He
loves me. He loves me.

(*Enter the Doctor, the Black Man and two Pressmen*)

DOCTOR Where's Mr. Brown?

FIRST PRESSMAN The ambulance is here.

SECOND PRESSMAN The police will be here any moment.

BLACK MAN Where is he?

HARLOT (*Racing to each of them and kissing them each in turn*)
He loves me. He loves me. He loves me.

Curtain

ACT TWO

SCENE ONE

When the curtain rises, three bishops are talking together. The original Bishop of the hillside is there and begins the conversation.

FIRST BISHOP I want to make it clear that I take no responsibility for this man. None at all. (*Looking at his watch*) I rather hope he doesn't come after all. He may not.

SECOND BISHOP Why not? You said you wanted us to meet him.

FIRST BISHOP Don't blame me if you don't like him. He's apt to say and do odd things. I don't want you to be shocked. He's not what used to be called—well, it's an old-fashioned way of putting it . . .

THIRD BISHOP You mean he's no gentleman?

FIRST BISHOP Exactly.

THIRD BISHOP I'm old-fashioned enough to like gentlemen.

SECOND BISHOP And dislike the rest?

THIRD BISHOP Not so. A bishop is meant to dislike nobody. That wouldn't be right. But I must admit I like somebody with my own sort of values. It makes everything easier. And there are so few of them left nowadays.

SECOND BISHOP (*Laughing*) You really are old-fashioned.

THIRD BISHOP Yes, I am. It's the last thing we dare to be. We sweat and strain to prove to everyone how modern we are. Very tiring, I find it. And it doesn't work anyway. Nobody believes us. But we have this great fear of anyone calling us out of date. We've got to be with it, whatever that means. (*Looking hard at Second Bishop*) So we organise dancing in our churches, and bingo parties in our halls. We try to cut Christ down to the size and shape that suits everybody. We encourage sex and people standing at the bars of pubs instead of sitting at our feet in pulpits.

FIRST BISHOP Most of us aren't like that.

THIRD BISHOP I know. That's the tragedy. Most of us are as old-fashioned as I am. We believe in prayer. We even believe in purity. We believe in looking after people's souls. We never raise our voices above the crash and rattle of the world. We distrust passion because we cannot control it. We go on doing a quiet job in a quiet way. But the modernists do all the shouting. A few loud voices seem to speak for us all. They make the news, and it's often the wrong news.

(*Enter Fourth Bishop, waving a newspaper*)

FOURTH BISHOP Have you seen the news?

FIRST BISHOP No.

FOURTH BISHOP It's about your friend, Mr. Brown.

SECOND BISHOP I hope he's been behaving like a gentleman.

FOURTH BISHOP (*Looking at the paper and reading with relish*) He's involved himself in some brawl in a public house. One man's dead. There's been fighting and drinking. The police have been called in. The paper says they're looking for him to ask him some questions. It all sounds thoroughly unsavoury.

SECOND BISHOP And thoroughly exciting.

FOURTH BISHOP (*Defensively*) I only thought you ought to know.

THIRD BISHOP If he's on the run from the police, surely he won't come here?

FIRST BISHOP (*Slowly*) I don't know. I have a horrid idea it's just the sort of thing he would do.

(*Enter Mr. Brown briskly and quickly. His hands are still bandaged, but the blood no longer shows*)

MR. BROWN Good afternoon, my Lords.

FIRST BISHOP Good afternoon, Mr. Brown. I'm glad you came.

(*The other Bishops look at First Bishop with some surprise*)

MR. BROWN Are you? Splendid.

SECOND BISHOP No need to call us "my Lords". We're quite ordinary people.

MR. BROWN Sorry if I called you the wrong thing. I get called so many things one way or another that I'm afraid I get a bit careless about what I call other people. But if you're ordinary people, why, may I ask, do you wear those extraordinary clothes?

(*The Bishops look at their gaiters and at each other*)

THIRD BISHOP (*Huffily*) It's an old-fashioned custom, Mr. Brown. And I venture to say, a good one. In the old days, when bishops rode on horseback, they had to wear gaiters to keep the . . .

(*He is about to make a well-rehearsed speech of explanation that has been given to many audiences many times*)

SECOND BISHOP The fact is that we wear these clothes to make men see we are not like other men.

MR. BROWN Aren't you like other men?

FOURTH BISHOP We're bishops.

MR. BROWN Yes. That I know. But if you're not like other men, you don't need different clothes for them to notice it. If you are like other men, all the gaiters in the world won't make you different.

FIRST BISHOP You seem to have been in some sort of trouble.

MR. BROWN Trouble? No. Not that I'm aware of. (*He sees the newspaper in the hand of Third Bishop, who has taken it from Fourth Bishop and is reading it*) Oh, you mean all that? Yes. They're looking for me now, I believe. It *was* a bit awkward for them. You see, there was blood on my hands when I left the place. One of the pressmen noticed it and told the police. An old wound. But I think I'm safe here, don't you? This is the last place they'd expect to find me. (*Sits down on a chair*)

THIRD BISHOP No doubt you meant well, but it was in

my view a mistake to mix with those sort of people. I tell you this for your own good. There are plenty of respectable folk around and, though I'm sure, Mr. Brown, you have a perfectly simple explanation to give the police when they catch you, you'd be wise to avoid bad company.

MR. BROWN (*Looking around him and smiling*) Well, at least I'm in good company here. No. I shan't explain a thing. The police will have to work it out. That's what they are for, isn't it?

SECOND BISHOP Why were you down there?

MR. BROWN Ask him. (*Pointing to First Bishop*) Two friends of his were there. They asked me to go along.

(*The other Bishops look at First Bishop with astonishment*)

FIRST BISHOP Friends of mine? You must be joking.

MR. BROWN The lady and gentleman who were with you on the hillside when we met. Surely you remember? They seemed to need a bishop badly down in that pub. Just the place for a bishop or two, if you ask me. But none of you were there. So I had to do the best I could.

THIRD BISHOP And a mess you made of it. All this publicity. All this deplorable vulgarity in modern newspapers. Disgraceful. Thoroughly bad taste, I say. (*Once more eagerly sticks his nose into the newspaper*)

SECOND BISHOP (*Drawing up a chair close to Mr. Brown. First Bishop and Fourth Bishop draw up closer around him also. It has the air of an inquisition*) Look here, Mr. Brown. We'd better make the most of our time. You must get away from here as soon as you can. You wouldn't want the police to find you here, would you?

MR. BROWN I don't know. On the whole I can't think of a better place. I'm sure it would help the police to meet some bishops. It might do something for you all to get to know the police.

FOURTH BISHOP You take this very lightly. We want to ask you a few questions.

SECOND BISHOP We want to discover where you stand in certain matters.

FIRST BISHOP You mustn't be upset if we seem abrupt. Time is short.

MR. BROWN I'm not pressed for time. There's plenty of it. But ask away.

SECOND BISHOP We can say things here that we could not say to everybody.

MR. BROWN Why ever not? Surely bishops live so their every word can be shouted from the rooftops for the benefit of humanity, and their every thought flashed on a giant screen for all the earth to see and wonder.

(*Bishops glance at each other. There is a short silence*)

FIRST BISHOP You have a high opinion of bishops.

MR. BROWN Some of them have a high opinion of themselves. I didn't dress them up like this, you know. But I do have a high opinion of what they are meant to be.

SECOND BISHOP We're living in modern times. You and I know, Mr. Brown, that the old ideas of God up in the sky are out of date. They served their purpose, I grant you. It was an image simple people could understand. But these spacemonauts and cosmonauts have been up and around, and, ha, ha, all come back saying there's nothing there. What do you think we should tell men now—about God, I mean?

MR. BROWN Tell 'em the truth.

FOURTH BISHOP What is the truth? Where do you think God is, Mr. Brown?

MR. BROWN What an extraordinary question for a bishop to ask anybody. I thought you were supposed to know things like that and tell others about them. But if you want my opinion, God is wherever anyone looks for Him. He's in you and me. He's up in the sky, whether the spacemen recognise Him or not. He's in their capsules with them, and down in the ooze of oceans, in caverns where dead sailors of the centuries are sleeping. He's in the Milky Way and in the muckheaps outside the cowsheds where beasts give milk. He's in stars and sewers, in sinners and saints, in mud and machinery, in every thought and every word in every heart everywhere.

SECOND BISHOP Surely, you don't suggest that the Almighty has time to be interested in every little detail of every life all day long?

MR. BROWN All night long, too. That's the trouble, you see. Men think God is like them. They can't care for everything everywhere. Their minds and hearts are too small. God can and does. That's the difference.

FIRST BISHOP Mr. Brown, where do you stand on sex?

MR. BROWN I was going to ask you that very question, Bishop. (*First Bishop looks up sharply and puts out a hand as if to stop him*) But as you asked me first, I'll tell you. It's like asking whether I'm for sun or moon or earth. They're there. So I'm for them. And I'm for sex. Strongly for it.

THIRD BISHOP Are you another of these modernists? These people who think that anything you want is what you ought to have?

MR. BROWN I'm more modern than any of you. But that doesn't mean I believe in all this nonsense about it being uncharitable to call sin sin and unchristian to try to cure it. No. I think that if God gave a man flesh and instincts, He can help him to control them. Don't you?

(*The Bishops look at each other*)

SECOND BISHOP Demonstrably false.

FOURTH BISHOP Look at the world. They have no sort of control of their instincts.

FIRST BISHOP Look at us.

MR. BROWN I am looking at you, just as you are looking at me. If you live straight yourself, you don't have to spend your time telling everybody else from the pulpit that what was once thought crooked is crooked no more.

SECOND BISHOP We have to move with the times. Public opinion has changed. People just won't accept the old versions of sin. They don't believe in it.

MR. BROWN People may not believe in motor-cars. But if they start crossing the M.1 with their eyes shut they'll get knocked over just the same. If you abolish a belief in sin, you abolish a belief in forgiveness and cure—you don't need either.

FOURTH BISHOP Exactly. And think how much happier everyone would be.

MR. BROWN Are they? Are you making them really happier? Come to that, are you?

SECOND BISHOP I flatter myself I live for something larger than mere personal happiness.

MR. BROWN Yes. You indicated just now that you were out to please public opinion, to move with the times.

FIRST BISHOP Aren't you?

MR. BROWN I'm out to change both.

SECOND BISHOP Where do you stand on things like divorce and families?

MR. BROWN I'm for the right kind of family and against the wrong kind of divorce.

FIRST BISHOP What exactly does that mean?

MR. BROWN For better for worse, for richer for poorer, in sickness and in health, till death us do part. It's as clear as glass and as definite. I neither stop short of it nor go beyond it. And as I'm with bishops, perhaps you'll allow me to say that you are all my family in so far as you do the will of my Father which is in Heaven.

SECOND BISHOP In so far as?

MR. BROWN (*Laughing*) No farther than.

THIRD BISHOP But I say, sir, that's cheating. It's almost blasphemy. It's quoting from the Bible. And then laughing at it.

MR. BROWN I wasn't laughing at it. I was laughing at *you*. You say you are old-fashioned. But if anybody takes the Bible seriously nowadays, some of you are the first to say they are out of date.

THIRD BISHOP Sir, that's a most offensive thing to say. We ask a few straightforward questions about God and you are rude in return.

MR. BROWN I tell you the truth. You interpret it as rudeness. It's not what most men expect of bishops. But it's better, I think, to let you know here and now that I don't believe in this god of yours.

SECOND BISHOP That's the most interesting thing you've said.

MR. BROWN (*Stands up and moves away to talk to them*) Yes. I thought you'd be interested. I don't believe in your sort of god with his watered-down ways and doubtful disputations, and theology designed to prove you needn't take him so seriously after all. I don't believe in a god so selfish that he helps to keep up these silly class concepts where a man is thought to be better because he went to one kind of school and talks with one kind of accent. Nor do I believe in a god so small that he justifies hating a man just because he's a boss or rich or happens to have something you want and can't get.

FOURTH BISHOP (*To the other Bishops*) This is wild talk. It's the sort of thing you hear on a tub in Hyde Park. It's Communism.

MR. BROWN Communism? Communism? It's become a word that's used more and more and means less and less, like Fascism. It's just a dirty word from people who don't understand it. Look here, you Bishops. Put yourselves up in the skies if you've got the imagination to do it. (*Mr. Brown leaps on a chair*) See yourselves there, looking down from Heaven on this torn, suffering, amazing, dangerous planet, to judge it if you can, to show mercy as you must, to pity and punish as you dare. Imagine the millions of hearts and faces turned to you up there in hope and prayer, and imagine millions of backs turned away from you in disillusionment and hatred. Here are the Communists teeming over half the earth. From their mother's milk they've been fed Karl Marx. They've been taught to hate God. They have no knowledge of Him except by stealth and instinct. They've murdered Him, or done their best to do it. But they've marched through blood, torture, misery to feed the hungry, house the homeless, put hope of something new into the hearts of humanity. Then there are the non-Communists with their strong sense of their own righteousness. They talk about God. Some of them even print "In God We Trust" on their money. Out of this half of the earth, with all their opportunities and protestations, have come two world wars in fifty years, the castor oil of Fascism, the gas chambers and Gestapo of Hitler, and the toleration of social and economic injustices that gave Marx his philosophy and Stalin his fuel and flame. They've been taught to fear God, but all they do is to flee from Him. Now you have the Christian West glorifying sex and satirising faith—rationalising the materialism that they despise and hate in their enemies. They've had the wealth. They've had the power. They've had the chance of faith. They've been entrusted, so they say, with the hope and truth of all ages. What have they done with it?

FOURTH BISHOP Stood on a chair before history shouting like you, Mr. Brown, and making themselves slightly ridiculous.

MR. BROWN (*Coming down*) I think you are right, my Lord. And like me, they are coming down.

SECOND BISHOP You over-simplify everything. Life is not right and wrong, black and white. It's a complicated, sophisticated society.

MR. BROWN I was talking to somebody not long ago who was sure there was nothing but black and white in life —but everyone white was devil and everyone black saint.

SECOND BISHOP Can't you be serious? Surely it's worth having a dialogue about these matters without making jokes.

MR. BROWN Well, I'll be serious. Serious enough to tell you I don't take your complications seriously. You complicate things to protect yourselves from reality. Life is more simple than men like you make it. You enjoy complicating everything. It gives you a sense of power. It lets you flex the muscles of your mind and impress the public with what they do not understand. You feel you are better than the rest of us with your long words and tangled theologies.

THIRD BISHOP Don't be rude. It's ungentlemanly.

MR. BROWN Forgive me for not being a gentleman. Treat me as a man. I like it better. A gentleman often camouflages beastly behaviour with his talk, and clothes and perfumes. But a man is different from a beast. Inside every heart two voices live and speak—a good one and a bad one. Men need to take time every day to throw out the bad one and let in the good. It's so simple that gentlemen are made uncomfortable by it. They resent it. They call it childish because they know it's true. A man will face truth.

SECOND BISHOP And what may I ask is truth?

MR. BROWN The truth is the right you deny and the wrong you justify. They are part of us all and you pretend there's no division between them.

FIRST BISHOP I don't know whether I have the imagination I need, Mr. Brown. But I have enough to know I will never pretend again. I've been wrong for years. I've never been honest. I've preached faith but lacked it. I've preached morality but refused to live it. I lost my way by calculated compromise and deliberate disobedience—by doing what I should not have done, but refusing to do what I should have done. I've soaked up flattery and vaccinated millions against catching the real thing. I'm a fraud. Mr. Brown, I'm sorry. I'll never be the same, say the same, do the same again. It's amazing to think that at my time of life even a bishop can see something new and start to be different.

THIRD BISHOP Disgusting. No gentleman would dream of saying such things. It's like undressing in public.

FIRST BISHOP It's only James v, verse 16.

FOURTH BISHOP (*To First Bishop*) Of course. What's the verse say anyway?

SECOND BISHOP Confess your faults, one to another.

MR. BROWN And pray for one another, that ye may be healed.

THIRD BISHOP We'll have to unfrock the fellow if he goes on like this. It's a disgrace to the Church.

FOURTH BISHOP He'll get over it.

SECOND BISHOP I hope he will. But it's this man (*Pointing to Mr. Brown*) who is responsible. He'll not only disgrace the Church. He'll destroy it, if we allow him to go on like this.

(*The door bursts open. The Harlot rushes in. She goes straight to Mr. Brown and seizes his arm*)

HARLOT There you are, dearie. I've been looking everywhere for you. You must come at once.

FIRST BISHOP What's happened?

HARLOT Police. (*Dragging Mr. Brown*) Come. Come quickly. (*To the Bishops*) Oh, do tell him to come with me, please!

THIRD BISHOP Yes. Go by all means. We can't afford any scandal here.

FOURTH BISHOP Yes. You'd better get away while you can.

FIRST BISHOP (*To Harlot*) Where will you take him?

HARLOT Never you mind. I've got a safe place for him. But I won't tell you where. I don't trust any of you.

SECOND BISHOP Get him out of here.

(*Harlot pulls Mr. Brown out of the door. He looks back and lifts his hand in salute to First Bishop as he goes*)

FIRST BISHOP I hope the police don't get him.

THIRD BISHOP My dear fellow, come and sit down and calm yourself. This emotionalism is bad for you. It'll only do harm.

FOURTH BISHOP (*Sitting down between Third Bishop and First Bishop*) Yes. And theologically, you know, he's hopelessly, dangerously wrong. You'll realise it as we talk things over.

SECOND BISHOP (*Still looking at the doorway through which Harlot and Mr. Brown left*) You fools. You don't understand what we're handling. We shall have to do something about that Mr. Brown.

(*The others look at him, astonished by his passion, as the curtain falls*)

Curtain

SCENE TWO

A street.   The Harlot, holding Mr. Brown's hand, comes across the stage, pulling him.

HARLOT Hurry!

MR. BROWN Do you want to run?

HARLOT Yes.

(*Mr. Brown stops dead in his tracks*)

MR. BROWN You seem as much in a hurry as that black man trying to get you up the hill. Now you want me to run away. But when the Bishop thought of running away from the Black Man with a knife, you called him a coward.

HARLOT That's different. Oh, do come on! You're such a fool. You don't know what you're in for. The police liked Andy. If they once get their hands on you they'll never let you go.

(*The Black Man comes in, with a knife in his hand, and sees them*)

BLACK MAN Ah! Here are the two lovebirds. I've been looking for you.

MR. BROWN With a knife in that big black hand of yours?

BLACK MAN Maybe. Maybe not. I'm just not sure.

HARLOT (*Standing in front of Mr. Brown, protecting him with her arms. To Black Man*) Keep back. Keep off. You shan't harm him.

BLACK MAN How do you know it's him I want to harm? It may be you, darling. But I want to ask our friend one question.

MR. BROWN What is it?

BLACK MAN Did you kill Andy?

MR. BROWN What difference will it make to you if I did?

BLACK MAN He's the only man who really stood up for me, and I loved him for it.

MR. BROWN You loved him because he fed your hate. You hate me because I feed your love.

BLACK MAN I loved him because he hated white men. I'd hate you more than I do if you weren't black.

HARLOT You're both out of your minds with this wild talk. Andy's dead and there's nothing to be done about it. Anyone can see that you (*Pointing to Black Man*) are black and he (*Pointing to Mr. Brown*) is white. There's nothing to be done about that either. Let's get on, dearie.

BLACK MAN (*Thrusting the Harlot away from Mr. Brown with one hand and holding up his knife with the other*) Stop. You shan't go until you have answered.

MR. BROWN Very well. The truth is that if anybody killed Andy, you did.

BLACK MAN Me? I never touched him.

MR. BROWN Not his body, but his soul. You taught him to hate. Hatred was the one place where he found success. He enjoyed the flattery of being the Black

Man's friend, the big White Chief of the Black Brotherhood. He liked you to think he was the one white man who understood. It made him purr like a pussy cat. And you went on stroking him. He bought your favour by abusing his own kind. He thought he'd please you by cursing me. He never learned the lesson of life that hate is hate and hate is wrong, and hate can be cured. You went on feeding his hate till his heart swelled with it more and more and more like a balloon. And it burst.

BLACK MAN Don't you hate? Didn't you hate me when I hit you?

MR. BROWN I don't hate anybody. It's childish. I hate some of the things they do, especially to themselves. I hate what you're going to do to me, but I don't hate you. I never will.

BLACK MAN I'm not going to do anything to you.

MR. BROWN You are, you know.

(*Black Man drops knife*)

BLACK MAN You devil. Leave me alone. I'm frightened. It's the first time I've been frightened. (*He runs away*)

HARLOT What's he going to do to you? He'll kill you if he can.

MR. BROWN *He* won't kill me. And it wouldn't matter much if he did.

HARLOT (*Tugging at him*) You've gone crazy. Come on, dearie. Do come.

MR. BROWN You worry too much about your life. It's

only a shadow, a flower, grass, wind, vapour, water spilt on the ground, a jet plane crossing the sky, a ship moving over the horizon, a thread cut by the weaver, a dream, a sleep, an awakening. Your life is nothing.

HARLOT It's not my life I'm worrying about—it's yours. Look here, dearie. Do you really love me?

MR. BROWN I do.

HARLOT Then come with me.

MR. BROWN All right. I'll come. And I'll never leave you. Remember that. Even when I'm not there, there I'll be. Even when you don't see me, I'll have my eye on you. No parting from now on. But I'm jealous. I won't share you with anybody. Understand?

HARLOT (*Tugging him*) Come on.

MR. BROWN You don't understand. But you will.

HARLOT Come on. Do come on. You need to rest. I'll take you to my place.

MR. BROWN You'll be safe there. I'm safe anywhere. But there's no rest for me yet.

HARLOT Do come on.

(*She drags him off as the curtain falls*)

Curtain

SCENE THREE

The curtain rises on the bar where the pressmen have been sitting. Nobody is there. It is late at night and not many lights are on. First Pressman comes in. He goes to the bar and bangs on it.

FIRST PRESSMAN   Hello there! Open up! Anyone at home?

(*No answer. He goes behind the bar and starts looking at the bottles. Enter Second Pressman*)

SECOND PRESSMAN   (*Dramatically*)   Got you.

FIRST PRESSMAN   You clown. Turn on more light if you know where the switch is.

(*Second Pressman goes over and lights up*)

Nobody's in. The bar's open. It's the chance of a lifetime. What'll you have?

SECOND PRESSMAN   The chance of a deathtime, you mean. Mine's a double Scotch. Make it treble if I don't have to pay.

(*First Pressman serves him*)

FIRST PRESSMAN   Treble coming up. What a night! Poor old Andy. He certainly made the headlines with his last story. If he were still alive, he'd be down here now drinking away to celebrate hitting the front page.

SECOND PRESSMAN   Perhaps he is celebrating. Free whisky was his idea of heaven all right. He could find more excuses for drinking Scotch than any other reporter I know. And that's a claim to glory. If he wasn't drinking to refresh his memory, he was drinking to try to forget something, or someone. He made drink into his *Encyclopaedia Britannica* and eraser all in one. Where's that girl of his, do you think?

FIRST PRESSMAN Probably the police have got her. (*Comes out from behind the bar*) But I'm taking no chances. If she finds me here handing out Scotch without charging for it, she'll break a bottle on my head. Thank God she's lost herself for once.

(*Enter Presswoman*)

PRESSWOMAN Who's lost? Not you two. If there's one place you are always at, any hour, any day, it's here.

SECOND PRESSMAN Who knows better than you, dear? And you don't come here just looking for us. That's certain.

PRESSWOMAN (*Sitting at the bar. Bangs on it*) Hello there! Open up! Customers waiting!

FIRST PRESSMAN Nobody there, dear.

SECOND PRESSMAN This is the one-and-only annual gift night, dear. Help yourself.

(*Presswoman goes behind the bar, fetches a bottle and siphon and glass, brings them out and sits at the table with the others. She talks as she does so*)

PRESSWOMAN Well, what do you know? Poor old Andy promised to stand me a drink every day for the last ten years. I never even got a cup of coffee out of him. Now he's doing us proud. Wish he could be here to share it with us. Here's to Andy! (*She lifts her glass and drinks. The others drink, too*)

FIRST PRESSMAN (*To Second Pressman*) Whoever suggested women were the weaker sex was nuts—or inexperienced. I'd never think anyone could be as frozen hard as this gorgeous bundle of femininity.

SECOND PRESSMAN She'll melt. You watch her after a glass or two. She'll be crying like a little child.

PRESSWOMAN The last time I cried was before the war.

FIRST PRESSMAN Which war, dear?

PRESSWOMAN Shut up. Do you suppose we'll have to work again tonight?

SECOND PRESSMAN Why the hell should we?

PRESSWOMAN The police may get Brown.

FIRST PRESSMAN They're sure to get him. But there's no more news in that.

SECOND PRESSMAN Relax, dear. Your night's work is done.

PRESSWOMAN It was an odd business. All that whisky into water stuff. What do you make of that?

SECOND PRESSMAN Nothing to make of it. I tasted the stuff myself. It was whisky all right. Andy was tight.

FIRST PRESSMAN He'd been tight before. It's the first time I ever heard him say whisky tasted like water.

PRESSWOMAN There was something odd about that character Brown. Very odd indeed. I didn't like him.

SECOND PRESSMAN Nor I.

FIRST PRESSMAN Nor I. And I can tell you why we didn't.

SECOND PRESSMAN Why not?

FIRST PRESSMAN He's the sort of man who would rob us
of our profession. You could feel it in him as soon as
you got within yards of him.

PRESSWOMAN No. That's unfair. He's not robbing us of
anything. He's given us a good story tonight.

SECOND PRESSMAN Nonsense. He had nothing to do with
it. Andy gets the credit. It's his story. Here's to Andy!

(*Once more they all drink*)

FIRST PRESSMAN I don't mean that. But Brown is the
sort of person who believes that the public should only
read what's good for them—and that he must decide
what's good. I could feel the hot breath of the censor
down my neck as I banged away at my typewriter each
time he looked at me. I could sense the long, sharp,
selective nose of interference poking like a pair of
scissors into my copy, ready to snip out any blasphemy,
violence, dirt, horror or sensationalism that comes our
way. It would cut my living-line. I'm against it.

PRESSWOMAN Doesn't sound like Brown. Sounds like
the dull aches of a long-buried conscience stirring in its
tomb.

FIRST PRESSMAN Don't you believe that. My conscience
and I parted company twenty years ago. I can't afford
the luxury of keeping one. You need to own a newspaper before you can keep a conscience for a pet in these

hard times. No. The public love reading what Brown would call bad for them. They swallow filth like Andy swallowed whisky. Materialism excites them. Goodness bores them to death. Brown is a bore. And a dangerous bore. I hope the police catch him and lock him up for a long, long time.

(*As First Pressman is talking, the Doctor and Second Bishop come in*)

DOCTOR   Very interesting you think Mr. Brown's dangerous. My friend, the Bishop here, was saying the same thing.

(*The Pressmen rise in some embarrassment*)

FIRST PRESSMAN   Do come in. Come and join us.

PRESSWOMAN   I'm afraid there's nothing here but whisky, Bishop. I'd make you a cup of tea or coffee or whatever it is bishops drink, if I knew where anything was around here. Maybe I can find some lemonade or something.

SECOND BISHOP   Whisky will do splendidly, thank you. I like it.

SECOND PRESSMAN   Help yourself, Bishop. (*Holding the bottle to the light*) The bottle's almost empty. (*To Presswoman*) Bring another bottle, will you? Drinks are on the house tonight.

(*Bishop and Doctor help themselves to drink and sit at the bar*)

DOCTOR   The Bishop and I are old friends. Indeed, he's what might be called my spiritual adviser. He came looking for me tonight when he read the story of Andy in the evening paper. He wanted to ask me a few questions about Mr. Brown. Apparently he's seen him.

(*The Pressmen and Presswoman are at once interested*)

SECOND PRESSMAN Where is he now?

PRESSWOMAN Did he come to confer or something?

FIRST PRESSMAN Were the police with him?

SECOND BISHOP He went off with some woman who seemed to know him well.

FIRST PRESSMAN That's a new angle.

PRESSWOMAN If it's that sort of woman it'll be curves not angles.

SECOND BISHOP I gained the impression she was going to try and hide him from the police. Will she succeed?

FIRST PRESSMAN (*Getting up*) Not a hope. You'll have to excuse me, I'm afraid. You have no idea, Bishop, where this girl lives?

SECOND BISHOP None, I fear.

(*First Pressman goes out, followed by Second Pressman*)

SECOND PRESSMAN We'll have to follow this up. I thought I was through for the night.

(*Presswoman rises*)

DOCTOR Do you go, too?

PRESSWOMAN Yes. I'd better go. These two boys will be telephoning all over town now. They'll be on to the police to see whether they know who the woman is. And if I know my editor, he'll be on to me to sit and write out what it feels like to be in love with a suspected murderer. As if I'd know.

(*She is moving out*)

SECOND BISHOP Good night. Good luck. And, if I may say so, it does you much credit to be so conscientious about your work. I hope they don't keep you up much later.

PRESSWOMAN Don't get me wrong, Bishop. I'm not going back to the office. I'm going to bed. And I'm going to my sister's house, where they'll never find me. Mr. Brown may be hiding from the police. I'm hiding from my profession. But both of us will be caught again by morning. Good luck. Good night. (*She goes*)

SECOND BISHOP I'd never thought of newspaper work as a profession before. But I suppose it must be one. Tell me, Doctor: if and when the police catch Mr. Brown, what will they do to him?

DOCTOR Nothing. What can they do?

SECOND BISHOP They say he's a murderer. Even in these modern times, the police do something about murderers when they catch them.

DOCTOR He's no murderer. Andy could have dropped dead any time. He just got tight and angry and pop! Then he went. The police will ask him questions, and from what I saw of this Mr. Brown, they'll get some funny answers. But they won't be able to hold him. They'll let him go.

SECOND BISHOP A pity. A great pity.

DOCTOR That sounds uncharitable and even unchristian for a bishop. What have you got against him?

SECOND BISHOP Brown's dangerous. Far better for everybody if he got into real trouble and was put away. He came to see some of us after this sad affair of Andy. He didn't seem troubled by it at all. But he troubled me. Yes. He troubled me deeply. I know the sort, you see. They crop up once every two or three hundred years—and there's no peace until they are in their graves. Sometimes no peace then. They leave seeds of violence behind them.

DOCTOR Did the other Bishops feel this way about him?

SECOND BISHOP (*Rising and walking up and down*) No. Between ourselves, my dear Doctor, they lack the intelligence. They didn't know what they had on their hands. You don't have to be exactly a super-egghead nowadays to become a bishop.

DOCTOR Nor any other day. Surely it's always been character more than brain, sanctity more than sense to make a great bishop?

SECOND BISHOP (*Startled*) Exactly. Precisely. But, you see, you gave me the key to this fellow Brown. It showed what sort of person is confronting us.

DOCTOR (*Laughing*) I'm glad I gave you any key, Bishop. But I was quite unconscious of it.

SECOND BISHOP You told me what happened in this very place earlier this evening. You repeated the exact words Brown said to that unhappy dead reporter. He said,

M.B.—G

"I'm for what's right and against what's wrong. And something inside each one of us can tell us how to decide."

DOCTOR That's about it.

SECOND BISHOP (*Excitedly*) Don't you see what it means? It's the breed that all down the ages has cut at authority and undermined the Church. It's unhappy Joan of Arc and her voices. It's Luther and his defiance. It's Hitler and his insanities. It's Stalin and his butcheries—all in the name of right. When once you get men like Brown saying they and God can decide what's right, what's wrong, you have the begining of barbarism. You have voices telling men to kill kings, to rape and spoil and plunder, to bomb factories, rob trains, steal other men's wives, terrify old women in the streets, overthrow governments, behave like savage animals. You run the risk of every man regarding himself as infallible and every woman mounting a white charger and galloping through the land screaming for debauchery in the name of liberty. You have intellectuals advocating nonsense—in the name of sanity—and professors propagandising philosophy, that can only lead to decadence and the death of freedom.

DOCTOR You seem to me to have a situation very like the one we have today.

SECOND BISHOP Far from it. We still have an Establishment that, with all its faults, holds society against disintegration with its authority and power. We have the law. We still have the Church, which yet stands firm in the track of Satan, watchful with the wisdom of centuries, strong with the strength of Christ.

DOCTOR What would you do to Brown?

SECOND BISHOP No nation can stand two governments in the land. Brown's beliefs mean that God comes before all human loyalty and every human authority— family, country, government, law, even church itself. When men start thinking they can communicate directly with Almighty God, the whole of society is threatened. As a bishop, I shall pray for his soul. If I were a statesman, I would destroy him.

DOCTOR Have you ever destroyed anybody, Bishop?

SECOND BISHOP (*Sitting down*) Forgive me for getting so excited. I haven't felt so strongly about anything since first I decided to refuse the chance of becoming a stockbroker like my father and to accept the calling of the Gospel. No. I can't think I have ever destroyed anyone.

DOCTOR I have. It's a grim business the first time you do it. But you get used to it. I don't know too much about God. I dislike what I know. And the rest of it I don't believe in. But I'm a sort of god. Every doctor has to be. I have to decide by myself again and again what is right or wrong—and live with the result, even if someone else dies.

SECOND BISHOP Whatever do you mean?

DOCTOR Old people suffer. They drool at the lips. They lose the power of limbs, speech, thought. They can't

stand up, sit down, wash, eat or move without help.
All they can feel is pain. Sometimes their families,
daughters, sons, wives, husbands come to me. They are
enslaved by old loyalties. Their whole lives are run and
ruined by dutiful care of a carcass that will be happier
when it's dead. They begin to hate those whom once
they loved. Some say doctors have to keep death at bay
at all costs. Sometimes I help him to stretch out a kindly
hand and bring relief to much human suffering. Do you
blame me?

SECOND BISHOP I prefer not to think of such things, not to
know about them.

DOCTOR But you must know about them, Bishop. After
all, if I'm responsible for your body, aren't you responsible for my soul?

SECOND BISHOP Go on.

DOCTOR It's so easy for us. (*He takes two small bottles out
of his pocket*) Here in one bottle are pills that will send
you to sleep and you will waken in the morning
refreshed and ready for the day. Here in the other are
pills that, in certain circumstances, will send you into a
sleep that lasts into the long, long silence. And I am
entitled by the power given me by law and your
Establishment to prescribe either. (*He puts the bottles
back in his pocket*) Think of infants born into the world
with hideous disabilities, with missing limbs or missing
faculties. Mental and moral tragedies that know no
human cure. One prick of my needle can end their
suffering and save those who love them lifelong sorrow.

Tell me, Bishop, is it ever right for me to decide to end life as well as save it? Or if I declared to you that I had often done so, would you say I was another Mr. Brown, a dangerous fanatic, ready to defy convention, law, customs, traditions, everything, to do what seemed best to me?

SECOND BISHOP I would not be prepared to answer your question.

DOCTOR Mr. Brown would. And I know what his answer would be: "Who are you, Doctor, to play the part of Providence? If you ask the Creator, He'll tell you to leave His creatures alone. God gives life. Man is not there to destroy it. Pain, suffering, the unselfishness of care for old and ailing people may be God's gift to develop love, charity, character, grace in others. Don't interfere with God, Doctor. Don't judge God, Doctor. It's dangerous, Doctor." That's what your beloved Mr. Brown would say.

SECOND BISHOP He's not my beloved Mr. Brown. But you certainly don't seem to like him.

DOCTOR I hate him. I hated him from the first moment I set eyes on him.

SECOND BISHOP Why?

DOCTOR Hate knows no "whys" any more than love. It's the hate of instinct that a terrier feels towards a rat.

SECOND BISHOP Or a rat towards a terrier.

DOCTOR Don't preach to me, Bishop. Spare me that. After all, it was you who told me that the man was dangerous.

SECOND BISHOP (*Slowly*) You aren't the police surgeon by any chance?

DOCTOR No. Why?

SECOND BISHOP I was thinking that if I were Mr. Brown and the police caught me, I should hate to be your patient. But if I were a man in charge of this country, it might be far the best.

DOCTOR (*Laughing*) He's not my patient. But you've answered the question you said you were not prepared to answer.

(*The door is pushed open. In comes the Harlot. She stops. Then calls over her shoulder*)

HARLOT It's all right. You can come in. There's one of you here already.

(*First Bishop enters. Second Bishop rises. Both Bishops stare at each other in amazement*)

BISHOPS (*Together*) I didn't expect to see you here.

HARLOT (*Going behind the bar*) No. It's the first time any bishop has ever been in this place. Two in a night is more than anybody could have expected, even the newspapers. (*She looks at the bar*) Been making yourselves at home, have you? Oh well, I don't blame you.

SECOND BISHOP I must be going.

FIRST BISHOP Do stay.

SECOND BISHOP No. Please excuse me. I don't want to meet your new friends. And it's better from every viewpoint that we are not seen or found here in this place together. One bishop here might charitably be supposed to be trying to get publicans and sinners into the Church. Two might seem to suggest that the Church was being induced to join the publicans and sinners. (*He goes*)

HARLOT Stuck up, isn't he? But I suppose most of them are. (*Comes round the bar to the Doctor*) All the same it's a bit of luck he's going. Because you were the one we were looking for, Doctor.

DOCTOR I find that hard to believe.

HARLOT It's true, honestly, isn't it, Bish? Tell him.

FIRST BISHOP The fact is that we are in some difficulty. This young lady knows where Mr. Brown is.

DOCTOR Have you told the police?

FIRST BISHOP No. She won't tell them—and she won't tell me.

DOCTOR It's your duty.

HARLOT Duty? Duty? All you men think about are words to excuse you doing the decent thing that costs something and pays nothing. Oh, won't you help? Do get him to help, Bish.

FIRST BISHOP The fact is that she thinks Mr. Brown is ill. He's been saying and doing very strange things today. I've noticed it myself. She came to find me and ask my advice. She mentioned that there was a doctor here at the time of that terrible accident this afternoon. She said you were often here late at night. So we came to find you.

DOCTOR What do you want?

FIRST BISHOP You had the chance of seeing Mr. Brown this afternoon. Did he strike you as normal?

DOCTOR Quite normal. Excited, perhaps. Strained by now, certainly, I imagine. But quite normal.

HARLOT Oh, he's not. He's not himself at all. He's talking about life being jet planes and vapour. He's talking about never leaving me and loving me. He's just wild. I suppose you wouldn't come and see him, Doctor— without letting the police know?

DOCTOR Certainly not. I daren't, even if I were willing. If the police get to hear of it, they'd ruin me.

HARLOT Whatever can we do? He'll sit up there all night long, without a wink of sleep, talking in that funny way of his that I can't understand half the time, and then the police will come and take him away. I don't know what to do.

FIRST BISHOP (*To Doctor*) I quite understand your position. I'm glad to have seen you. I just wanted your assurance as a medical man that Mr. Brown is not a mental case or anything of that kind. Probably nothing wrong that a good night's sleep won't put right. But I'm afraid the poor fellow's unlikely to get it if what this girl says is true.

DOCTOR (*Thoughtfully*) A good night's sleep? A good night's sleep? Now that couldn't do anybody any harm, could it? Everybody needs that. Yes. I think I might be able to help you there.

HARLOT Would you? Something that will make him sleep for a night and a day and another night perhaps? Till the police get fed up and I can smuggle him out of town.

FIRST BISHOP We must let the Doctor decide on the proper thing. I imagine one good night is all that's needed. It's an unusual request, Doctor, but it would be kind of you to help. The young lady would be most grateful. So would Mr. Brown, I'm sure.

HARLOT (*Rushing over and kissing the Doctor*) Oh, Doctor, you're a darling. Can you help? Will you help?

DOCTOR (*Slowly*) I rather think I can.

Curtain

SCENE FOUR

The Harlot's house. There is a huge double bed in it. Mr. Brown is sitting in a dressing-gown reading a newspaper. The Harlot comes in with First Bishop.

HARLOT Not asleep yet? You should have slept hours ago.

MR. BROWN Oh, it's you. I didn't feel like sleeping. I can do without it. Where have you been?

FIRST BISHOP Down at the pub. It's the first time I've ever been inside one.

M.B.—H

MR. BROWN I expect the police will be here soon.

HARLOT Nonsense, dearie. They don't have a clue where you are. Do they, Bishop?

FIRST BISHOP Not a clue.

HARLOT How do you feel, dearie?

MR. BROWN I feel fine.

HARLOT You'll feel finer.

MR. BROWN What are you going to do for me?

FIRST BISHOP We've got something for you to take. The Doctor gave it me down at the pub. He says it will help you to sleep and you'll wake up feeling far better.

MR. BROWN I couldn't feel better, if I tried.

HARLOT Don't try, dearie. Just relax. And take the medicine. There's a good boy.

FIRST BISHOP You've had an exciting day. You need time to recover.

MR. BROWN I don't much want your medicine.

HARLOT Look here, dearie. You say you love me. Take it for my sake. Will you?

MR. BROWN (*After a pause, in which he looks at Harlot and Bishop*) All right. For your sake, I'll take it. You're sure you know what you're doing?

HARLOT Of course we know. There. Get into the bed. We'll tuck you in, won't we, Bishop? No need to worry. We'll be here when you wake up in the morning.

(*She runs out of the room and comes back with a glass of water, while the Bishop helps Mr. Brown off with his dressing-gown and into bed*)

Here you are. Here are the pills. Here's the water. Drink up.

FIRST BISHOP Yes, drink up.

MR. BROWN (*After a pause*) Are you quite sure?

FIRST BISHOP Quite sure.

HARLOT Quite sure.

MR. BROWN Very well. (*He takes the pills and drinks*)

HARLOT That's a good boy. (*Takes the glass*)

FIRST BISHOP We'll let you sleep now.

HARLOT We'll be in the next room waiting.

(*As they go quietly to the door, Mr. Brown speaks from the bed*)

MR. BROWN Bishop.

FIRST BISHOP Yes?

MR. BROWN Would you pray? I think I'd sleep better if you prayed.

FIRST BISHOP It's not a very suitable place really.

HARLOT Oh, pray away, Bishop. Don't mind me. You'd be surprised. Lots of them do, some before and some after. I can never make head or tail of it. But somehow it seems to suit them.

FIRST BISHOP Oh well. (*He kneels. The Harlot waits, leaning against the door*)

HARLOT Hurry up, though. We want you to have your sleep now, dearie.

(*Bishop begins to say the Lord's Prayer, "Our Father . . ."
When he gets to the phrase, "Thy Kingdom come. Thy will
be done on earth as it is in Heaven", Mr. Brown joins in, in a
loud voice, from the bed. He sits up*)

MR. BROWN That'll be the day.

HARLOT (*Hurrying forward*) There, there. Relax. Don't get excited. It's rude to interrupt praying. Even I know that. You musn't do it. Really.

(*Mr. Brown lies down again*)

(*To Bishop*) Finish up now. Quickly. We must let him get his sleep.

FIRST BISHOP (*Still on his knees*) Very well. (*He starts the Lord's Prayer again. Mr. Brown joins in at first. But his voice grows faint and finally dies away*)

HARLOT Sh! He's sleeping. Come on. Let's leave him.

(*They tiptoe out. The stage grows dark. There is a muster of music. Suddenly a hubbub breaks out in the next room. You hear the Bishop's voice*)

FIRST BISHOP'S VOICE Officer. Officer. Don't make this noise.

HARLOT'S VOICE Damn you. You betrayed him, damn you. Dirty swine!

POLICEMAN'S VOICE That's enough of that. (*Sound of scuffle*)

BLACK MAN'S VOICE He's in there. I know the place well. That's where he'll be.

POLICEMAN'S VOICE Let me get by, if you don't mind, sir.

(*There is a knock and then a louder knock on the bedroom door. The policeman comes in, followed by Black Man and Bishop, followed by Harlot held by another policeman.*

POLICEMAN Turn on the light.

(*Black Man turns it on*)

BLACK MAN (*Pointing to bed*) There he is. I told you.

HARLOT Leave him alone.

POLICEMAN (*Going over to the bed*) Mr. Brown! I say, are you Mr. Brown?

(*When there is no answer he starts shaking Mr. Brown*)

Mr. Brown. Wake up, sir. Wake up.

(*He bends down and looks more closely. Listens to Mr. Brown's chest. Then shakes his head at the policeman holding the Harlot, pulling out notebook*)

(*To policeman holding Harlot*) Better call an ambulance, Joe. There's not much more we can do here. Now, if you don't mind, I'll have to ask a few questions.

(*Black Man rushes to the bed and stands shaking Mr. Brown furiously, shouting, "Mr. Brown! Wake up, Mr. Brown!" at the top of his voice*)

Now stop all that. It won't do any good. I've seen too many of them.

BLACK MAN (*Falling on his knees. Still shaking the bed*) Mr. Brown! Can you hear me? Listen to me. I didn't mean it. I didn't mean it. Come back. You must come back. Say you understand. Say you know I didn't mean it.

(*The Harlot puts her hands to her mouth and starts screaming, looking at the bed, as the curtain falls*)

Curtain

SCENE FIVE

A street, with Pressmen, Doctor, Bishops passing by. A newsman is selling papers.

NEWSMAN   Murderer kills himself! Escapes police by seconds! Read all about it.

THIRD BISHOP   (*Reading paper, to Fourth Bishop*) I never read these dreadful newspapers as a rule. But it's interesting to see what has happened to somebody we were speaking with so recently.

FOURTH BISHOP   (*Looking at paper*) He was in a bed in a brothel.

THIRD BISHOP   (*Snatching paper*) Disgusting. Let me see. Degrading.

FOURTH BISHOP   Revolting.

THIRD BISHOP   Disgusting. (*They pass on*)

FIRST PRESSMAN   What a story!

SECOND PRESSMAN Andy would have loved it.

FIRST PRESSMAN I wonder if he knows what's going on.

SECOND PRESSMAN If he's in Heaven, Andy will be too drunk to know.

FIRST PRESSMAN If he's in the other place, he'll be too busy greeting old friends to care.

SECOND PRESSMAN Good old Andy. (*They pass on*)

SECOND BISHOP (*To Doctor*) Just what I'd have expected him to do.

DOCTOR I wonder where he got the tablets?

SECOND BISHOP I wonder.

DOCTOR Probably the best thing that could have happened.

SECOND BISHOP Providential. Simply providential. That's what I call it. (*They pass on*)

(*After a moment, the Harlot and First Bishop enter, hurrying. They buy a paper. They start reading it as the newsman still crying his wares passes on. The Harlot for the rest of the play speaks with her old fun but with new authority.*)

FIRST BISHOP It's horrible.

HARLOT Do you think so, Bishop? I don't. I think it's glorious.

FIRST BISHOP Don't talk like that. It's jarring.

HARLOT Just what you need, you and your crowd. A good jarring. But it's glorious just the same. You see, we're the only ones who know.

FIRST BISHOP Know what?

HARLOT Know what really happened.

FIRST BISHOP I wish I knew what really happened. I am still perplexed and shocked.

HARLOT I'm happy.

FIRST BISHOP How can you be?

HARLOT How can't you be? Look at the paper, Bish. (*She holds it out to him*) Nobody says who Mr. Brown was. See?

FIRST BISHOP Well, who was he?

HARLOT Now, Bishop, surely it's your job not mine to answer questions like that?

FIRST BISHOP (*Slowly*) I don't know who he was.

HARLOT It's a new day, Bishop, when you say you don't know a thing like that. I thought somebody like you would put on a parsonical voice and tell me he was Christ or something.

FIRST BISHOP I wouldn't say that. I would not dare say it. The consequences would be unbearable. Think of what happened. Think of what was done to him.

HARLOT Yes. And we're the ones who did it. Now, look here, Bishop. My hide's tougher than yours. Women can bear much more than men. In a man's world we have to. We do our best by putting on men's trousers and encouraging the men to wear long hair like ours. But it's a silly business really. If you can't tell me who Mr. Brown was, then I'll tell you.

FIRST BISHOP Be careful. I'm not sure I want to hear it.

HARLOT Well, you're going to hear it whether you like it or not. You're a Christian, aren't you? Well, to a Christian, Brown was Christ. Of course he was. They treated him in that pub and in your Bishops' conclave, and in that room last night just the way Christians always treat Him. They bullied Him down from the Cross till they got Him under their feet. Then they trampled Him to their shape and size. They tried to put Him safely into a package with their label on it. When He would not wear it, they denied Him and destroyed Him.

FIRST BISHOP I'm not sure what you are saying, but I think it's blasphemy.

HARLOT It's not. I'm not really much of a Christian, Bishop. In fact, I don't know whether you would call me one at all. So I can't blaspheme. All I know is that I just love Mr. Brown and I know he loves me. He seems something wider, bigger, far more wonderful than the sort of Christ your church gives folk like me. He was for everybody everywhere in the world, for you and for me, for white and for black, for the people who talk about God and deny Him, for those who know nothing of Him but stretch out their hands in the dark. You know, Bishop, in him was the thing everybody hates when first they meet it—the best that a man or woman can be. I learn a lot from my profession. Men talk to me. They talk about their wives. Mostly, they complain of their goodness, not their badness. Their wives make them feel how rotten they are. That's why people hated Mr. Brown. He made them feel so rotten.

FIRST BISHOP You loved him.

HARLOT Yes. But it was different for me. You see, I needed to feel rotten. I knew enough about the wrong sort of love to recognise the real thing when I met it. So few people do.

FIRST BISHOP The Black Man doesn't. Poor chap, he must be feeling awful. It's a terrible thing to find out one day that you've been blaming somebody else for the failure of us all—the failure of humanity. We are all to blame. That's what Mr. Brown said, didn't he?

HARLOT That's better.

FIRST BISHOP What's better?

HARLOT You're thinking about somebody else besides yourself.

FIRST BISHOP It's extraordinary. I'm supposed to help people like you. But you're helping me. I was so certain of everything. Then, when Mr. Brown died, all grew dim and doubtful once again.

HARLOT You've a better mind than mine, Bish. But I think I have a bigger heart than you. You intellectuals are all the same. You argue yourselves out of the Kingdom of Heaven—then think you can argue yourselves back again. But you can't. Until your heart's in it, your mind will always wobble in and out. You need love, the right sort of love. I just love Mr. Brown. I don't have to think about it all the time. I just do it.

FIRST BISHOP I'd like to help that Black Man.

HARLOT Well why not? Mr. Brown told us to look after each other. He wouldn't waste time talking like this. I know exactly what he would do now. And we have got to do it together. Come on Bishop. (*She tugs at him*)

FIRST BISHOP Come on, where?

HARLOT We have got to find the Black Man.

(*They pass on as the curtain falls*)

Curtain

SCENE SIX

It is the three-tiered hill again, as at the start of the play. The stage is empty. Then the climbers appear. This time the Harlot comes first. She climbs with steadfastness, mounting to the second tier. Then First Bishop appears. Last of all the Black Man.

BLACK MAN I remember, this is the place where we rest.

HARLOT Not on your life. No rest for us.

FIRST BISHOP (*Laughing*) It's funny.

BLACK MAN What's funny?

FIRST BISHOP Last time we were here, you were telling us all to hurry and she was telling us all to rest.

BLACK MAN (*Sitting down*) The hate's gone out of me.

It's like the spring of a watch that's broken. All I can think about is, will he forgive me? Does he understand?

FIRST BISHOP He understands everything. You didn't kill him. (*Pointing to Harlot and himself*) We did.

BLACK MAN You did? Why did you do it?

HARLOT We didn't know what we were doing.

FIRST BISHOP Oh yes we did. At least, I did. I was trying to get rid of Mr. Brown for years before I put him to sleep last night. With my arguments and rationalisations and endless selfishness, I cut him down to size where I could handle him. I did him far more harm with my lovelessness than you did with your hate.

BLACK MAN Do you think he's up there? Or is the whole thing just a dream, a mystery of misery, a fake?

FIRST BISHOP He's there.

BLACK MAN You seem so sure.

FIRST BISHOP I am sure.

HARLOT I've got a bone to pick with him. That's why I want to get up there.

FIRST BISHOP What bone?

HARLOT He said he'd never leave me. But he has.

FIRST BISHOP You know he hasn't.

HARLOT What makes you say that?

FIRST BISHOP I can see him every time I see you. You're utterly different. You're ten years younger, a thousand years wiser. The odd thing is, so am I. Experience is

the bridge between doubt and certainty. I doubted all
my life. Five minutes of honest obedience instead of
dishonest rationalisation of disobedience—and I felt
faith born in my heart, as real and lovely and growthful
as a baby in a womb.

BLACK MAN I wish I could have faith. Obedience to who
or what? How do you obey what you don't believe in?

FIRST BISHOP You obeyed your hate. But you didn't
believe in it, did you?

BLACK MAN I always knew it was wrong, if that's what
you mean. But I enjoyed it.

FIRST BISHOP It wasn't altogether wrong. You hated
the right things. But you hated the wrong people.

BLACK MAN Who should I hate?

FIRST BISHOP Nobody. It only makes them worse. It
doesn't change them.

BLACK MAN But I enjoyed my hate.

HARLOT There you are. It's the same for us all. We do
what's wrong because we enjoy it. Then we start
saying it's right. And then we start to believe there's no
such thing as right and wrong.

FIRST BISHOP And that's the end of faith. But the fire of
faith always beats the fire of wrath in the end.

BLACK MAN Maybe. But the fire of wrath beats no fire
at all. Hate's like a hammer. You wouldn't understand. But a man like me needs something to hit his
enemies. He's lost without it.

FIRST BISHOP Hit your enemies with love.

BLACK MAN How?

FIRST BISHOP I don't fully know. But I'm learning. Supposing you and I hate together every evil thing on earth but love together the evildoers, and plan for them so intelligently and persistently and passionately that they either change—or kill us?

BLACK MAN Why, Bishop, dying with a man like you would almost be a pleasure. What's come over you? If love does that to a man like you, heaven help our enemies.

HARLOT You men always talk about enemies. You hit Mr. Brown. Was he your enemy?

BLACK MAN No. I hit him because he was so damned right. He threatened my hate. I couldn't bear it.

FIRST BISHOP He threatened our have-and-hold religion. We couldn't bear it either.

HARLOT He didn't threaten anything except my living. And I loved him for it. Come on. Let's get up there and see him. We'll only settle this when we can talk to him again.

BLACK MAN I can't go on. I just can't go on any farther. But I want to see him again more than anything on earth.

FIRST BISHOP I'll give you a hand. Come on. Let's try.

(*He goes back to the Black Man. Puts an arm around his shoulders. The Harlot starts to come down again*)

HARLOT I could go ahead. But I'm not going without you. Somehow it's all or none now. I don't think he'd be too pleased to see us without you. You see, it's rubbish to say we're all islands or whatever it is. No man is an island today. We're all one big body with wounds, scars, warts, colours, hopes, hates, fears and feelings. One more big break will bleed us all to death. You see, we need each other.

BLACK MAN Being needed is something different from being used.

FIRST BISHOP Helping is different from hating.

HARLOT Giving you a leg up is different from smacking each other down.

(*The two of them help the Black Man up to the second tier.*)

BLACK MAN Can't we have a rest? You can't heave me up the whole way.

FIRST BISHOP We can try.

(*As they link arms once again to tackle the third tier, the light grows brighter. The Bishop and Black Man do not notice. They are preparing to scale the last height. But the Harlot sees. She looks up, shading her eyes with a hand. Then she points and shouts with triumph*)

HARLOT There! Look! We're all right now. There's Mr. Brown. I knew he'd be there. He's coming down to help us.

(*As they all look up the hill, the curtain slowly falls*)

Curtain